W9-ACI-821

DATE DUE

BROADWAY

BROADWAY
A Play

By

PHILIP DUNNING
AND
GEORGE ABBOTT

27-26372

GEORGE H. DORAN COMPANY
on Murray Hill   :   New York

BROADWAY
— A —
PRINTED IN THE UNITED STATES OF AMERICA

PREFACE

Have you ever sat on a hillside so high above a little town that you could look down on its toy-like spires, its nursery-red rooftrees, its fantastic curling smoke, its spider-web of streets and footways and, so sitting, have you noticed how its myriad faint sounds hum a kind of gentle, homey tune—the tune of that little town?

Some ears are so acute that, even at a blurring distance, they can separate the violin notes from the cellos, can hear the French horns sharp and clear and pluck the harp-strings out of all the chords the orchestra would blend. Such a one, surely, was Lewis Dodd, the oblivious pagan who strides through the pages of that brilliant novel "The Constant Nymph." Dodd and his new, uneasy bride are loitering on such a hillside above a little fishing-village with the twinkle and scurry of small boat-lamps marking out the devious line of the Mediterranean shore far below them.

"Lewis!" she complains, "Stop throwing stones! I don't believe you've listened to a single word I've been saying!"

"Yes, I have. You were talking about jugs. I'm listening. I'm listening to you and a dozen other things as well."

"There aren't a dozen other things. There's only

. . . the chapel bell, and some men shouting in the boats down on the quay . . . and a dog barking, and some ducks in the garden below."

"Not bad! You've missed about fifty larks in the sky, and the grasshoppers all around us, and a car changing gear on the hill, and the oars in the rowlocks of that boat putting out, and the children playing, and the goat bells away on the hill behind us, and I think I can hear a smithy."

"What a babel it sounds! I'd have said it was a quiet evening."

"So it is. It's so quiet that you can hear every sound in it. Generally there's too much noise for that."

To such ears as his, I suspect that each town in the world must play its own concerto and that, blindfolded, he could be led to each high hill and say: "This is Avignon" or "This is Seattle." To the average listener on the Palisades, "there's too much noise for that."

But at midnight, the hubbub of commerce dies down, the snores of the sober and toil-worn sink to an indistinguishable hum and then, sharp and clear, New York plays a cruel, crazy tune of its own. It was given to the men who compounded this jaunty, gamin melodrama called "Broadway" to distill it from the syncopated, defiant, mocking sounds a-quiver in the golden haze that hangs at midnight above the centre of the island of Manhattan. Of all the scores of plays that shuffled in endless procession along Broadway in the year of grace, 1926, the one which most perfectly caught the accent of the city's voice was this play named after the

great Midway itself, this taut and telling and tingling
cartoon which, produced with uncommon imagination and
resource, was presented to New York at the Broadhurst
Theatre on the night of September 16, 1926.

The theatre is at its best when it is journalistic, when
it makes its fable and its parable out of the life stream-
ing down its own street, when the pageant on its stage
is just such a cartoon and criticism of the land and day
lying across the sill of the stage door. So journalistic
is "Broadway" that, on the night when it was new in
New York, I ventured the suggestion that its manuscript
could scarcely have been delivered through the ordinary
snail-paced channels. It must have come in over the
ticker. So journalistic is "Broadway" in the pell-mell
millrace of this era that I doubt if a Rip Van Winkle
who had dropped off to sleep the night of the première
of "Within the Law" back in 1912 and awakened just
in time to attend its logical successor at the Broadhurst
fourteen years later, would have understood or believed
any of its entirely plausible plot, would have recognized
half the words spoken in the argot of its people or
would have experienced without painful shock the greater
freedom of speech and the more honest natural history
which, in the age of the New Candor, lends character
and substance even to the plays concocted to entertain
the multitude.

Indeed, when, in the last month of 1926, a company
set sail from New York to play "Broadway" in London,

I think the management must have itched to send a
lecturer on ahead of the show. Just as Professor Clay-
ton Hamilton now goes ahead of Mrs. Fiske in "Ghosts"
to get the provinces mentally adjusted to the demands
of an Ibsen tragedy, so it would have been no bad thing
to send some Burton Holmes to lecture on the fantastic
new folkways of Manhattan Island lest London think
the authors of "Broadway" had invented the nightmare
panorama of passion and prohibition and politics which,
as a matter of fact, does not tell the half of it.

ALEXANDER WOOLLCOTT.

CAST

(As played for the first time at the Broadhurst Theatre,
New York)

NICK VERDIS..........................*Paul Porcasi*
ROY LANE.............................*Lee Tracy*
LIL RICE.........................*Clare Woodbury*
KATIE ....*Ann Preston*
JOE ....*Joseph Spurin-Calleia*
MAZIE SMITH ....*Mildred Wall*
RUBY ....*Edith Van Cleve*
PEARL ....*Eloise Stream*
GRACE ....*Molly Ricardel*
ANN ....*Constance Brown*
BILLIE MOORE ....*Sylvia Field*
STEVE CRANDALL ....*Robert Gleckler*
DOLPH ....*Henry Sherwood*
"PORKY" THOMPSON ....*William Foran*
"SCAR" EDWARDS ....*John Wray*
DAN McCORN ....*Thomas Jackson*
BENNY ....*Frank Verigun*
LARRY ....*Millard Mitchell*
MIKE ....*Roy R. Lloyd*

Gangsters, Waiters

THE SETTING

We are looking at the rather gaudy side room of a night club. There is a carpeted stairway at left, a heavy oak door with a grated slide peek-hole in it, just below the stairs; at the back double doors, now closed, lead to a private party room: on the right, double doors open into a hallway running at right angles—the hall is three feet wide and across it swinging doors lead into the cabaret proper. Nick's office is at the extreme right.

There is a piano, poker machine, wall phone and a number of red chairs.

BROADWAY: Act One

Broadway

The rising curtain discloses the orange-lit, tinsel magnificence of the private party-room at the Paradise Night Club. To the tinny obbligato made by "Lil" Rice at the piano, five chorus girls are in line singing and dancing one of the numbers from the revue. The rehearsal is under the direction of Nick, a middle-aged Greek, mercenary and hard.

LIL, the prima donna of the cabaret, at the piano,— a heavy, middle-aged woman with a certain amount of good looks, which, however, have long since lost their bloom. She rolls her own, and removes tight slippers from swollen feet whenever occasion permits.

ROY LANE, a typical song and dance man, with his coat off, sleeves rolled up, is leading the number. The chorus girls, MAZIE, GRACE, RUBY, PEARL, and ANNE are in line behind ROY.

Some of the girls are in street clothes, others in practice clothes. One or two have their skirts pinned up so as to give their legs freedom for the dance. Some of the girls' coats, hats, wraps,

15

etc., are hanging on hooks or thrown on chairs or tables.

Joe, an Italian waiter, enters from cabaret, takes pin-wheel effect to cabaret.

Nick

(*As they dance*) Hey, straighten your line—You. Straighten it up. Now, listen, don't forget to smile. Pearl—some pep. (*Girls continue to dance in straightened line*) (*Joe has returned to carry out spot-light*) Shake it, shake it. (*Shouts*) No, no! stop! (*They all stop guiltily*) Pearl, watch what you're doing.

Pearl

(*Under her breath, as she turns away*) Go fry an egg.

Roy

(*To Pearl*) You went into that step on the off-beat, girlie.

Nick

(*To the dancers*) For God's sake, think what you're doing, will you? Now once again,—the finish.

Lil

Where from?

Roy

(*Singing the cue music*) Ta da-ta-tadada-ta-ta.
(*They finish the dance—and break formation. The orchestra is rendering dance music in*)

16

the cabaret. This continues at intervals throughout the play. Colored lights play upon the swinging doors)

Nick

(As they stand waiting for a decision) No good. Nothing like it. It ain't only you dance with your feet, you gotta smile—show the teets—— *(He illustrates)* Last night—oh—hoo. *(Makes a noise of disgust)* Rotten. (PEARL *and* RUBY *start to whisper)* Pearl, you pay attention. *(They both look away, awed)* I say, smile. Show the teets I say. Like this.

Roy

I guess you got it now, ain't you, girls?

Mazie

Sure, we have.

Nick

Last night a gentleman gets up in the middle of the first number, he says to me, "Outside your place it says: 'Paradise Club—Best Cabaret in New York' —that's what it *says*"—and then he walks out.

Lil

Wise crackin' rounder——

Ruby

Had to be smart.

17

Nick

He was right. This show ain't bad, it's lousy.
Say, look—I pay you—and I can't even look at it.
The show's too tame—I have to undress you. Live
it up——

Roy

The show is good—what there is of it, Boss,
but you ought to get in more people.

Nick

Yeh?

Roy

(*Crosses to Nick*) Sure. *Variety* says the Golden
Slipper is doing a nifty biz but they got fourteen
weenies and six performers. Now, if you ask
me——

Nick

Well, I don't ask you—I don't ask nobody, y'understand?

Roy

Well, if you don't want good advice, that's your
loss.

Ruby

Anyhow, I should think you might save some of
your raspberries for the one that caused the whole
trouble.

Pearl

That's what I say.

Grace *and* Ann

Yeah. That's what I say.

Mazie

Hey, easy.

Roy

(*To them*) Nix, nix.

Ruby

How can we get it right if Miss Billie Moore don't take the trouble to come to rehearsals?

Roy

(*Under his breath*) Hey, don't be a kibitzer.

Ruby

Who the hell does she think she is—keep us waiting for her?

Roy

Well, I tell you, Mr. Verdis, I don't think she knew there was a rehearsal.

Ruby

She was standing right alongside me in the dressing room last night, when you called it.

Roy

No, she had gone.

Mazie

Certainly she had.

Ann

No, she heard it—she was in the room.

Grace

Sure. I saw her.

Mazie

You're crazy—I say she was gone.

Lil

Oh, for God's sake. (*They stop their clatter and look at her*) Listen, you poor bunch of baby saps— if you spent half your time minding your own business instead of watching other people——

Roy

So says I.

Lil

When I was your age before I got fat—yeh, fat— I kin say it myself—I was so busy tryin' to get somewhere, trying to get out of the chorus, I didn't know whether anybody was in the dressing room or not. If you're going to rehearse this, do it. If you ain't, tell me, 'cause I ain't supposed to sit here and pound this music box—I sing here and I'm just doing this for Nick.

Ruby

You ain't so fat you can't talk—are you——

Lil

(*Starts to get up*) Say, listen, Owl, I'll pull all the sawdust out of you if you ain't nice.

Nick

Here, here, here, what is this—Lil is right—Gals today ain't nothin' but a lot of jumpin' jacks. Come on,—we'll do it again.

Grace

Oh, please—I'm tired.

Nick

You're tired! My God, I got better girls in a dump once.

Roy

Aw, quit ridin' 'em, will ya, Mr. Verdis?

Nick

Ah, shut your face. I run this place.

Roy

They been rehearsin' since 8:30 tonight——

Ruby

Yeh, and don't forget we can't get this right 'till Billie gets here.

Ann

That's what I say.

Pearl

Why make us the goat?

Grace

How am I gonna give a performance . . .?

Nick

Quit it. I don't need no advice what to do with girls that come late.

Roy

Listen, Mr. Verdis, Billie's only been in this game a short while——

(JOE *enters with a drink for* NICK)

Nick

And she won't be in it a hell of a while longer. As soon as she comes in, she goes out. (LIL plays *"How dry I am."* NICK *pauses as he is about to drink and looks at her*) Joe, get Lil a drink.

(*He drinks. The girls lounge about the room, smoking, using nail files, etc.* JOE *exits to Hall*)

Roy

Gee, Mr. Verdis, it's not like Billie to fall down on the job. Why, that kid is one of the best lookers and neatest workers you got. You'll make one big mistake if you let her out—she's a mighty nifty little trick.

Nick

Why all the talk? You don't work for her—you work for me.

Roy

God knows I know that.

Nick

Whadda ya mean?

Roy

Well—not to pin any bouquets on myself, but where could you get a guy to do what I'm doing for the coffee-and-cake money you're paying me?

Ruby

He's off again.

Roy

You see it ain't only I can dance, but I got personality——

Mazie

Huh!

Roy

Personality plus——

Mazie

(*To Grace*) Ain't he a darb?

Grace

He hates himself.

Nick

Somethin' else ya got is a terrible swell head.

Roy

Who, me? Nothin' swell headed about me, Boss —I coulda been that way long ago, if I'd wanted to.

(KATIE, *a cigarette girl, enters down hall*)

23

Nick

Cut out the belly-achin' and quit anytime you want.

Katie

Mr. Verdis——

Nick

Don't bother me. Can't you see I'm busy?

Ruby

In conference.

Nick

What? (*He glares at the wrong girl. Then turns back to* Katie) Well, why don't you go?

Katie

It's for Mr. Crandall.

Nick

(*Manner changes*) Oh—well—he ain't here yet —who is it? Who wants him?

Katie

Them two same gentlemen that was in last night.

Nick

All right, I'm coming out. Tell 'em I'm coming. (Katie *exits down hall*) Don't you go to your dressing room till I come back—we ain't done rehearsing yet. (*Exit down hall*)

> (Ruby *thumbs her nose at his back and the girls break into a clamor*)

Ann

Gee, it's about time.

Grace

He's a slave-driver.

Mazie

Thank God.

Pearl

Don't he ever get tired?

Roy

(*Getting on his coat*)   Oh, lay dead.

Grace

Oh, gee, I can't rehearse any more.

Ann

Well, you're gonna have to, whether you can or not, so don't start squawking about it.

Ruby

Aw, I think I'll quit this dump anyhow.

Pearl

I'm gonna buy everybody a drink.

Ann

Big hearted.

Lil

My God, it can talk.

Pearl

What?

Lil

That's the first time I heard you speak since you been working here—I always supposed you was a deaf and dumb girl up to now.

Pearl

I worked in night clubs before—it don't pay to talk too much.

Roy

Like to see anybody stop me talking.

Mazie

So would I. (*They all laugh*)

Grace

Say, what about this drink?

Pearl

Does he let you have the waiter come in here?

Ann

Sure—Joe can go anywhere.

Grace

Come on, girls, let's go down the hall to the bar——

Ruby

Wait a minute—Maybe Pearl don't have to pay for mine. Four to one—a dollar or nothing.

> (*Puts coin in poker machine; pushes lever and watches the numbers spin. Is disappointed.*
> Ann, Grace, Ruby *and* Pearl *start out hall*)

26

Pearl

(*To* Lil)   Ain't you coming?   (Roy *waves her aside*)

Lil

They're bringing mine.

Mazie

I gotta 'phone.

(*The girls exeunt*)

Lil

Where the hell is Joe with my drink—he must be down in the laundry making it.   (*Picks up a copy of "Variety"*)   If your girl friend gets late to another rehearsal like this, she's gonna get a piece of my mind.

Roy

They must be some good reason why Billie ain't here.   Listen, Lil, don't put it into Nick's head to give her the air, will you?   'Cause she needs the do-ray-me pretty bad—she's got a mother and sister over in Trenton.

Lil

I never knew a jane in this business that didn't have.

Roy

On the level, I met 'em.

Mazie

I room with her and I happen to know she's a good kid.

Roy

And believe me, it pays to be good.

Mazie

Sure, but not much.
    (*Searches telephone book for her number*)

Lil

(*Wisely—to* Roy)   So you met the family, eh?

Roy

Yeh, I went out there one Sunday. You see, I take a sort of brotherly interest in that kid.

Lil

Brotherly?——

Roy

You heard me. Anyhow I and her are fixing up a little vaudeville act together.

Lil

Say, sweetheart, why don't you get hep to yourself?

Roy

What do you mean?

Lil

Ain't you wise that she's given you the bum's rush? Why, that guy's got her so dizzy she don't know you're alive.

Roy

Who? Crandall? No, no, not at all. She'll get
over that. She ain't used to going to such swell
places, that's all. She's got more sense than to care
a thing about Crandall himself, personally—it's just
the buggy ride—I seen it happen lots of times—
young kids get taken out by a rich guy—everything
swell; music, lights—they get baffled, you know
what I mean, dazzled—and then suddenly they get
wise to themselves that the whole works is a lot of
boloney and they realize where the real guys in this
world is at——

Lil

Hoofing in cabarets.

Roy

Yeah. That's no kid neither. (MAZIE *grunts derisively and crosses to phone*) Billie's ambitious to
get ahead in this game. (MAZIE *drops a nickel in
phone box*) I guess she'd want to stick with somebody could learn her something, huh?

Mazie

Pennsylvania 5000.

Roy

Her and me ain't long in this joint anyhow. I'm
going to make her something besides a chorus girl.

Lil

What's coming off?

29

Roy

As soon as I get Billie ready we're all set for a lot of nice booking on the big time.

Lil

Soon as you get Billie ready? Are you—all ready?

Roy

Who—me? Well, that's a funny question—you're lookin' at me every night. You can see. I don't belong here.

Mazie

Pennsylvania 5000.

> (JOE *enters from hall with drink.* LIL *throws cigarette on floor and steps on it preparatory to taking drink*)

Joe

I couldn't find Pete and he had the keys—that's what kept me.

Lil

That's all right. The longer it stands, the better it is. It was only made this afternoon.

Joe

Not this stuff. That's last week's.

Mazie

Operator, I want Pennsylvania five—— (JOE *exits to hall*) What? I did give you my nickel.

30

(*Placated*)　Pennsylvania 5000.　(*Sits on the back of the chair—her feet on the seat*)　Wonder if we could get Pullman service with this phone.

Lil

(*Offering glass*)　Want a piece of this?

Roy

No—I can't drink and do what I do.

Lil

(*Drinking*)　I see.　You ain't never played any of the big time yourself, have you, Personality?

Roy

No—but you know as well as I do—it's just the breaks.　Look at all the loafers in this man's town —getting by—have they got anything on me?　I ask you, have they?　This big Greek Nick is always cracking about Jack Donahue—there ain't a thing that guy's doin' that I can't do—yeh—and mebbe I done some of those steps first—but Jack got the breaks and mine ain't here yet.

Mazie

Pennsylvania 5000.

Roy

Listen, when I was out on the Gus Sun time couple years ago—the manager in McKeesport comes back to my dressing room and tells me—that

31

never did anybody do the stuff I was doing . . . and
the road show of the Follies was only there the week
before.   But the act with Billie is a sure thing.   And
then you'll see the old names—with a big ad in Variety, telling 'em—look who's here.   God, I dreamed
about it years.

Mazie

Pennsylvania Hotel?   Listen, I want to speak to
Mr. Manuel Tellezar——

Lil

My God, you can't find a guy with a name like
that in a hotel—he's in Ellis Island, dearie.

Mazie

Oh, for God's sake——   (*Hangs up in disgust*)
    (BILLIE *enters back door.   She is a beautiful
    little creature, despite the obvious common-
    placeness of her clothes.   She enters breath-
    lessly*)

Lil

Here she is now.

Mazie

Where you been, kid?

Roy

Gee whiz, Billie——

Billie

Is Mr. Verdis sore?

Lil

Oh, no, nobody's sore—just curious.

Roy

He was kinda sore till I talked him out of it. He may say a little something, but don't pay no attention to him. Where the hell you been?

Billie

Mr. Crandall said he'd keep track of the time.

Lil

Hah!

Roy

Oh, him.

Mazie

You been out with Steve?

Billie

I didn't think there was anything wrong.

Mazie

There ain't.

Roy

(*Referring to corsage of orchids*)   Did Crandall give you them dandylions?

Mazie

Listen, Billie, if you was out with Steve, you got nothing to worry about cause Nick won't dare say a word to you.

Billie

I didn't mean to be late, honest, I didn't—but it was just so wonderful and the orchestra was playing special numbers that he asked 'em to play just for me—and it just seemed like I was in a dream or something.

Lil

And ain't it hell when you wake up?

Billie

I just don't know where the time went, that's all. Roy, here's some more coupons.

(*He accepts the cigar coupons sulkily and adds them to a large roll which he carries in his pocket held together by a rubber band*)

Mazie

(*Looking at the phone*) I wonder if that banana gave me a phoney name.

Billie

When Mr. Crandall asked me to go to dinner with him, I told him I had a rehearsal and he promised to get me here on time.

Roy

Where is the big stiff?

Billie

(*Resentful of his tone*) He's outside parking the car.

Roy

I guess maybe it's time I give you a piece of advice, Billie—lay off these sugar daddies—I seen a lot of these big cabaret spenders—they're only after one thing.

Mazie

(*Walking toward phone*)   I wonder if that banana did give me a phoney name.

Roy

Don't let your head get turned by a lot of soft gab —bowing you out of a taxi like you was Texas Guinan or somebody. Don't think that—say, where do you s'pose he got his money anyhow?

Billie

In Florida real estate.

Lil

Listen, Personality—what difference does it make in this man's town where you get the sugar so long's you got it?

> (RUBY, ANN *and* GRACE *enter from hall.   At*
> *sight of* BILLIE *they splutter out their indig-*
> *nation*)

Ruby

Oh, so you finally showed up, eh—Say, you got a nerve.

Ann

That's what I say.

35

Grace

What d' you think we are?

(PEARL *enters from up hall*)

Billie

I'm awfully sorry.

(NICK *enters from down hall*)

Nick

Well—so—you did come—What you got to say for yourself—no, don't say it. Of all the dam' nerve ——

(STEVE *appears in back door. He is a tall man, handsome in a hard sophisticated way. He wears dinner clothes*)

Steve

Evening, Nick.

Nick

(*His manner changing to one of deference*) Well, look who's here. Good evening, Mr. Crandall, glad to see you.

Steve

Hello, girls.

Girls

Hello.

Steve

Hello, Lil. (*She bows grandly*) Hope I didn't keep Billie from rehearsal, Nick.

Nick

I was just gonna ask her where she was——

Steve

Guess it didn't put you out much.

Nick

No, no, it didn't make so much difference.

Ruby

(*Bitterly*)   I should say not.

Nick

What?

Ruby

I didn't say a thing.

Billie

(*To girls*)   Gee, I'm awfully sorry.

Nick

You and me can talk about that later.

Lil

Well, are we going to rehearse some more or ain't
we?   I been sitting here for three hours and my feet
hurt like hell——

Nick

Billie can rehearse separate with Jack Donahue
here.

Roy

No trouble at all.

37

Nick

So that's all for the rest of you.

Ruby

Thank God.

Steve

Oh, by the way, I'm tossing a little party tonight, and I'd like to have you all stay.

(*The girls crowd around him except* PEARL *who starts toward stairs*)

Mazie

That's us.

Ann

Sure, we will.

Grace

You tell 'em.

Ruby

Yes, we'll come.

Steve

How about it, Pearl?

Pearl

(*Pausing*) I don't think I can, Mr. Crandall.

Steve

You old cross-patch, I got some Chicago friends just dying to meet you.

Nick

She'll be there.

38

Pearl
Sure, I'll be there.

Steve
Fine. I can get the party room, can't I, Nick?

Nick
Anything you say, Mr. Crandall.

Steve
Bye, bye, little one, and thanks again for a very pleasant evening. (*He kisses her hand gallantly.* Roy *turns aside and gives him the bird, vaudeville fashion—a derisive noise made with the lips. The girls snicker.* Steve *looks around, not quite sensing what has happened.* Nick *hastens to dismiss them*)

Nick
Come on now. Get made up, girls. (*They start towards stairs. He turns to* Steve) Dolph and Porky are outside waiting for you.

Grace
Gawd, I'm all in. I'm going to hit the hay to-night——

Ruby
If you was a rich man's darling, you wouldn't have to rehearse.

Mazie
The trouble with you is, you're jealous cause he don't take you out no more.

Ruby

(*Pausing on stairs*)   Say, where do you get off to jump me?

Mazie

If you don't stop passing remarks about Billie, I'll jump you all right—I'll knock your block off.

Ruby

You and who else?

Lil

Shut up. Why don't you two hire a hall? (*Pushes past them*)

    (ANN, PEARL, GRACE, LIL *and* RUBY *exeunt upstairs*)

Steve

Tell 'em I'll wait for 'em here——
    (NICK *exits down hall*)

Mazie

I'm going to bust everything God gave her some night—all but her teeth. I'll take them out and give them back to her dentist.
    (MAZIE *and* BILLIE *exeunt upstairs*)

Roy

(*Who has been standing watching Steve*)   Have a nice ride this afternoon?

Steve

(*After looking him over, amused*)   Lovely. Sorry you weren't along.

Roy

Say, tell me something, will you?

Steve

Shoot.

Roy

I been knocking around cabarets, dance clubs, vaudeville, everything, for a long time, and what I can't get through my head is this—why is it that all the guys like you are never satisfied with the hundreds of janes that will do anything you want—all the rummies and bums you can have, and by God —you'll quit 'em all to go after one girl that you know is good—why is that, huh?

Steve

Do you know some that are good?

Roy

I know one that's good.

Steve

Who is that?

Roy

That's Billie.

Steve

You're sure she's good?

Roy

I'll give you odds she is.

Steve

Where the hell do you get the idea that no one can speak to this Moore girl but you? Who are you? What can you do for her?

Roy

(*Almost pleading*) I can do a lot for her, Mr. Crandall. I can put her in the Palace Theatre—inside six months.

Steve

Doing what?

Roy

Doing a swell dancing act. Now there's my cards on the table, Mr. Crandall, that's what I'm going to do for her. We can't lose. She's got looks, a shape, and with my personality——

Steve

Your personality. Oh, I see, that's what you're going to sell. Well, Kid, that's a great idea—just an idea. By the way, I guess I'll have you do a little clowning for a few minutes for my friends to-night—I'm not inviting you to remain on the party, understand, because there won't be dames enough to go round—I'll give you a ten spot.

Roy

Sure. I'll do some stuff I ain't done here seeing how you want some laughs.

(NICK *enters down hall, bringing* DOLPH, *a dark wiry man, and* PORKY, *placid and bald headed—both in evening clothes.* ROY *sees them coming—starts upstairs*)

Dolph

Hello, Steve.

Steve

Hello, boys. Get Joe in here. Nick, let's have a drink.

(NICK *goes up hall*)

Dolph

(*Kidding* ROY) Well, if it isn't old Fred Stone himself.

Roy

That ain't no insult neither. For his own kind of stuff, he's a hundred percenter, that guy—we can all learn something from him, believe me, even the best of us.

Porky

Yeh, but I like your stuff much better.

Roy

That's all right. Just keep your eye on me. Pretty soon you'll see my name in lights. It's in the boy,—I can't lose. (*Exit upstairs*)

Steve

Never leave any strychnine around, that guy is

43

just dying to commit suicide. (*They laugh*) The poor nut.

Dolph

I got the bracelet, Steve.

Steve

Good. I'll look at it later.

Porky

Let's sell this load of stuff to Nick——

Steve

(*Warningly*) All right——
(PORKY *stops abruptly.* NICK *enters up hall*)

Steve

(*Casually*) For Christ's sake, Nick, where's all your chairs? (*They all hasten to get him a chair*)

Dolph

Here you are, Steve.

Nick

We moved them back for rehearsing. It's all your fault, too, keeping that gal out all day.

Steve

Ain't sore, are you, Baby?

Nick

A lot good it would do me. (*They all laugh*)

44

Porky

(*As they sit*)   Had a lucky break last night, Nick.

Nick

Yeh, you fellas is always lucky.

Porky

I'll say so.

Dolph

Got hold of some great stuff.

Nick

Yeh?

Dolph

You bet, fresh from the boat.

Nick

(*On his guard*)   Didn't know you had any boat coming.

Porky

We didn't. . . .

Dolph

But Scar Edwards did.   (*They laugh*)

Nick

(*Protesting*)   This high-jacking is no good.

Dolph

But it's luck for you just the same, eh, kid?

Nick

I don't know—some day you get in trouble.

Porky

Let Steve do the worrying about that.

(JOE *enters with drinks*)

Dolph

Ah, here we are.

(PORKY *holds nose and gulps it down*)

Dolph

If Steve wasn't a big-hearted guy, he'd never sell you this stuff at the same price.

Nick

Good, eh?

Dolph

It's the real thing, Nick, no kid.

Nick

No, I got quite a lot on hand.

(JOE *exits*)

Steve

You got nothin' but cut stuff. You better get in on this—white horse in the clear—not white mule neither—you can get twenty bucks a quart for it.

Nick

No, they drank bum stuff so long they don't know when it's good. Anyhow, if I take booze you hi-jacked off Scar Edwards, he'll come down here and raise hell.

46

Steve

I'll take care of Scar.

Nick

If you fight with his mob—then I'll get it in the neck. Of course they won't make no trouble if you keep below 125th Street.

Steve

Roll over—trade is where you find it.

Dolph

You tell 'em.

Steve

My connections are better than any man in this town.

Dolph

You bet you.

Steve

In that same we got people on our list with streets named after them.

Porky

That's no lie either.

Steve

You don't think I'm going to let a greasy lot of Polish second-story men tell me where to head in, do you? I'm telling you that I want to clean up this order quick and I think I got a right to count on you.

Dolph

Sure. Where would you be today if it wasn't for Steve?

Porky

Yeah,—a waiter.

Steve

Never mind that—where would you be, as far as that goes?

Dolph

Ain't that what I'm sayin'?

Steve

It ain't what you was—it's what you are. I cleaned spittoons in my time, fella, and I'm proud of it—that's when Porky tried to make a box fighter out of me, eh, Porky?

Porky

I always said you had stuff in you—and now I'm workin' for you.

Steve

Say, boys, this business of peddling booze is the second largest industry in the United States right now—give me a year more at it and we'll all retire.

Nick

Listen, Steve, I'm on your side.

Steve

Well, good God Almighty, would I be sitting here talking to you if I thought you wasn't?

48

Nick

But the Edwards gang might shoot things up.

Steve

(*Quietly*) They ain't got a monopoly on it, have they?

Porky

Oh, Nick—— (*Waves him laughingly away*)

Nick

You're too quick with the gun, Steve; sometime you might get in trouble.—Anyhow, it's no good, a lot of murders—very bad for business. Scar might get me raided again——

Steve

(*Hard*) Listen, Nick, you never got poor taking my tips yet——

Porky

Damn right he didn't.

Steve

And I wouldn't advise you to change right now.

Nick

Oh, no. (*Depreciating the idea vehemently*)

Steve

Listen, Nick, if my trade is going to grow I got to crush a little competition now and then—I'm taking Scar's booze when I can lay my hands on it, and I'm taking his territory. It's just business, that's all. Are you with me or not? You gotta declare yourself in or out.

Nick

All right—send me what you want—I'll pay for it.

(JOE *enters, gets glasses, exits*)

Porky

Now you got sense.

Dolph

Sure.

Steve

Now, Nick, this party I'm giving is for the Chicago gang that hits town tonight. They're all itching to show what they can do, and if Edwards starts anything they'll be very handy—see.

Nick

Well, I'm counting on you.

Steve

Sure, you can count on me, cause I got everything fixed. Now, Porky, you go to the hotel and as soon as the gorillas land, get 'em dressed up and bring 'em around.

Porky

Sure.

Steve

I want all the girls to stay. Make it right, and tell Joe champagne, flowers and all the rest of it.

Dolph

Hot dog!

Nick

Anything you say, Steve.

Steve

Now go down the cellar and check up your stuff and see if you can't make this order a record, eh, old timer?

Nick

(*Crosses to hall door*) Anything that's for you, I want to do it. Come on, Porky— (*Peeks through doors*) Not so good for Friday night.

(PORKY *and* NICK *exeunt to hall*)

Dolph

(*As they are out of hearing*) That's the way to handle him, all right. He's got a nerve to argue after all you've done for him.

Steve

Well, we'll spend a lot of money tonight anyhow —make Nick feel good. Let's see the bracelet.

(DOLPH *passes it and stands watching*)

Who owned it?

Dolph

The fence wouldn't tell me. But he says it was lifted off one of the classiest mammas in town.

Steve

How much?

Dolph

Five yards. He wanted a grand at first. I beat him down.

Steve

All right—we'll keep it. It'll look nice on the kid—eh, Dolph?

Dolph

You tell 'em. You certainly have fell for that baby, ain't you? (*Plays poker machine*) I never seen you waste so much time on a jane.

Steve

(*Coolly*) Don't see too much.

Dolph

(*Apologetically*) You know me, Boss.

Steve

Got to handle each one different. Wouldn't want me to show my technique first thing, would you?

Dolph

Not if you mean what I think you mean.

Steve

This gal is a nice kid.

Dolph

She won't be after she knows you long.

Steve

That's all right too. (DOLPH *plays poker machine*) But you gotta use your head.

Dolph

Jesus! This machine is crooked.

(SCAR EDWARDS *enters back door. He is a tense man — slightly overdressed in Broadway fashion*)

Steve

You see, she don't belong in this cage at all— consequently you got to treat her different.

Dolph

(*Turning and seeing* SCAR) Well, for God's sake.

Steve

Hello, Sweetheart.

Scar

How are you?

(DOLPH *closes cabaret doors*)

I thought this is where I'd find you.

Steve

What made you think that?

Scar

Do you think Steve Crandall's the only bird in town that's got ways of findin' things?

Steve

Well, I'll tell you, Scar, I wouldn't advise you to do it often.

Scar

No?

Steve

No. In fact, I think you got a hell of a nerve to come bustin' in this way.

Scar

Not much busting about it.

Steve

Next time, knock—see——

Scar

You don't always knock when you come to visit me.

Steve

I don't visit you, Scar.

Scar

You visit my neighborhood sometimes, don't you, Steve?

Steve

Do you own it?

Scar

All depends on how you look at it.

Steve

I'm just telling you for your own good, Scar— Come gumshoeing in the back way of a strange place, you know, somebody might take you for a burglar.

Scar

(*Closes in*) I ain't scared of you guys. I come down here to have a showdown—alone—with no gun. (*Pats pocket to show he is unarmed*) So let's talk turkey.

Steve

All right, Edwards, but listen to what I tell you—next time you better let us know when you're coming or you may wish you'd brought your gun.

Scar

You don't let me know when you're coming.

Steve

Meaning what?

Scar

I s'pose you don't know.

Steve

You heard me ask you.

Scar

Aw, you know goddam well what I mean—you been poaching on me, Steve—you been cutting in on my territory and it's got to stop.

Dolph

Will you listen to that——

Steve

You own everything above 125th Street, do you?

55

Scar

We stocked that territory and we got a right to it.
My mob worked for four years to get things the
way we got 'em—and nobody—get that—nobody is
goin' to cut in from down here and spoil a nickel's
worth of it. You hi-jacked another truckload last
night (STEVE *rises*), yes and you been spillin' more
jack round for protection than we can afford—we
ain't never come down here to horn in on your
Broadway trade but you're ruinin' our game up there
and I'm here to tell you that you can't get away
with it.

Steve

If you knew me a little better, you'd know that
yelling wouldn't get you much.

Dolph

That's just what I was going to say.

Scar

Peddle your papers, will you. (DOLPH *walks
away squelched. In the cabaret the orchestra can
be heard playing George Olsen's Battle Number*)
I'm talking to the boss now. I come here for a
show-down with you guys, see.

Steve

All right. I don't mind a little show-down myself
once in a while. You're looking for trouble, is that
it?

Scar

No, I ain't lookin' for trouble. Nothin' like that.
Not that my friends ain't capable of holding up
their end, if it comes to that. But I say they's
plenty of business for everybody and them what
works up the trade should be the ones to get it.

Steve

And supposing I say that I'll sell any damn place
I can get away with it?

Scar

Then I'm warning you that it's dangerous for you
to do business in Harlem cause from now on 125th
Street is the dead line. Get me?

Steve

Yeah?

Scar

Yeah.

Steve

Well, that's just dandy, Scar. Thanks for the
tip-off. Now if you've spoke your piece you can
take the air. I don't care about having a public
fight with the likes of you because everybody in this
place don't know my business yet, and I don't care
to have you stand around and broadcast it.

Scar

There's a lot of things I can broadcast, if I have
to.

Dolph

(*Comes to the other side of* SCAR) You heard what the boss said, didn't you?

Scar

You too—the both of you—since you're looking for tips, I'll give you another one. I happen to be the guy who can clean up a few murder mysteries in this town. I suppose you don't know who knocked O'Connell off!

Dolph

What are you talking about?

Scar

And who dumped his body up in Harlem so my mob would get blamed for it?

Steve

What the hell are you driving at?

Scar

This is what I'm driving at——

Dolph

Wait a minute.

Scar

I've waited long enough. Now get this—You guys stay down here in your own territory and you leave my trucks alone. See—cause I got the dope on you, Steve—you croaked O'Connell.

Dolph

(*Grabbing his arm*)   Look here.

Scar

Take your hands off me or I'll bust your God-dam face. You guys can't put me out of business.

(SCAR *is facing* DOLPH. STEVE *quickly pulls out his gun, presses it against* SCAR'S *back and fires.* SCAR *pitches forward.* DOLPH *catches him in his arms.* SCAR'S *hat falls off*)

Dolph

Jesus Christ, Steve, what have you done?

Steve

(*Remaining cool*)   Get hold of him under the arms—quick—walk him out of here——

(ORCHESTRA *still playing battle number—trumpets and shots.* DOLPH *takes one of* SCAR'S *arms and* STEVE *the other and they start to walk him out as they would a drunken man*)

Wait a minute.

(*Gets* SCAR'S *hat, puts it on* SCAR'S *head. As* STEVE *and* DOLPH *are walking the dead man toward back door under stairs,* ROY *and* BILLIE *come downstairs from dressing room in costume*)

59

Roy

Come on, I'll run through the number with you—
we got time.

    (BILLIE *and* ROY *look over railing and see*
        STEVE *and* DOLPH *with* SCAR *between them*)

Roy

Who's the drunk?

Steve

Just one of the boys we're helping home.

    (SCAR, DOLPH *and* STEVE *exeunt back door,*
      closing it after them)

Roy

It's powerful stuff Nick dishes out.

Pearl

    (*Appears at top of stairs*)   Billie, was there a
shot?

Roy

(*Laughs*)   That's the band——

Billie

They're doing the battle number——

    (ORCHESTRA *just finishing Battle Number*)

Pearl

I'm nervous as hell tonight.

    (*Exits to dressing room*)

Roy

(*To* BILLIE) Come on now. Ready—let's do it together—1-2-3 (*They dance*)

> (NICK *enters from hall and stands watching* BILLIE *and* ROY. BILLIE *senses his presence and stops dancing*)

Billie

You didn't want to see me, did you, Mr. Verdis?

Nick

I did—but now I don't—all the same you shouldn't miss that rehearsal——

Billie

I'm awfully sorry.

Nick

Don't let this happen some more.

Billie

I won't—thank you, Mr. Verdis.

Nick

See if you can dance better tonight.

Billie

Yes, sir.

Roy

She will. I just came down to skate it over with her. (*He takes off coat, revealing the fact that his*

*cuffs are sewed into the coat sleeves and that he is
bare armed and a bit ragged underneath)* One-two-
three-four——

(NICK *exits to office*)

Billie
Wasn't he nice to me though?

Roy
Sure, he was afraid he'd lose me if he gave you
the gate. The last step, where you went into the
side kick, is where it got muddled last night. Now,
I'll count it slow—watch me——

> (*He hums the tune and they both dance as he
> counts—1-2-3-4—*BILLIE *gets mixed up on
> one of her kicks*)

No—no—that's where you went wrong last night.
Second time you do it with the left foot. Ready—
again—go——

> (*They do the dance again—this time correctly*)

You can't wish a number on—you got to rehearse 'em.

> (*She does the dance alone while he hums and
> counts*)

Fine. That's it. You just keep picking up a little
each day and improving and you'll be going fine before long—you'll be as good as I am soon——

> (*She demurs*)

Honest. Then we'll tie the merry old can to this saloon, eh, kid?

Billie

I s'pose so.

Roy

What do you mean—I s'pose so?

Billie

Well, that's what I mean—only Mazie says not to count on it, that's all. She says, well, I s'pose she's just kiddin'—but she says it's a pipe dream.

Roy

Yeh, no wonder she never gets anywhere with that kind of a outlook, huh?

(*She limbers up, putting her foot on piano and bending down to it*)

That's right, don't forget what I told you. (*He takes her by the back of the neck and helps*) The act is just as good as booked and you'll make a great partner too. We'll soon be copping three hundred a week—one hundred for you and two hundred for me. You could send fifty or so home to your old lady every week instead of ten.

Billie

I hope it comes true.

Roy

(*Puts on his coat*) Comes true? It's just as good as if I was handing you the money right now.

63

(*She stops exercise and starts toward stairway*) Is
that all you're going to do? Say, Billie, you're still
strong for the act, ain't you?

Billie

Sure, why not?

Roy

Well, you been wasting quite a lot of time lately.

Billie

Oh, I don't know.

Roy

We used to get in early and have a special rehearsal. Now you been staying out to dinner with
some guy or other.

Billie

Well, I don't mean to do what's not right—I'll
rehearse—only a person ought not to miss wonderful opportunities. I mean, I ought not to miss a
chance to go out with Mr. Crandall.

Roy

You ought not to miss a chance to go out with
me neither.

Billie

Well, of course, you're different.

Roy

I'll say I am. (*Imitates* STEVE) Bye bye, little
one. Thank you for a very pleasant evening—huh.
That's the parrot's cracker—that stuff.

64

Billie

Mr. Crandall has been very nice to me— (Roy *grunts*)—well, he has, Roy—and I don't like you making fun of him.

Roy

Well, I don't like him interfering with our act.

Billie

He isn't. I'll rehearse any time you say.

Roy

It ain't only a matter of rehearsing—you gotta keep your mind on your work. Don't be thinking about hotels and things like that—be thinking about your partner.

Billie

Well, I do.

Roy

Do you? Say, Billie, suppose we go out after, tie on the feed bag and talk over the act, huh?

Billie

Tonight?

Roy

Oh, I remember this is the night you go home to see your old lady, ain't it?

Billie

Well, this is the night I usually do.

Roy

Give her and your sister my love. By the way, Maloney Brothers are breaking in their new act over

in Trenton the last half; if you see 'em around, tell
'em I was asking for 'em.

Billie

Well, I don't know that I'll go.

Roy

(*Clouds*) Oh.

Billie

I thought maybe I ought to stay to Mr. Crandall's
party.

Roy

Can't they get soused without you?

Billie

Mr. Crandall asked me first one of all—he said
it would be just flat and stale without me.

Roy

That would be tough. Pardon me, while I laugh
(*Holds up his sleeve and laughs into it artificially*)
ha-ha. (*Resumes the serious tone*) I'm tellin' you
to go home—suppose anything ever happened like
your old lady kicking the bucket.

Billie

(*Walking away*) You would!

Roy

Listen, Billie, tell me something straight, will you?

Billie

Sure.

Roy

Are you falling for this guy?

Billie

(*Stalling*) I never thought of such a thing.

Roy

Are you falling for anybody?

Billie

Mr. Crandall never thinks of me that way at all.
He just considers me like a friend or just a kind
of pal.

Roy

I suppose he's going to adopt you. Just a big
brother. You wait a couple of days and I'll give
you the low-down on him. I'm gonna do a little
detective work myself. Florida real estate—hah!

Billie

Now, Roy.

Roy

I'm thinking of your career, that's all.

Billie

(*Flirting*) Is that all? I thought you might perhaps be thinking about me.

Roy

I take a personal interest in you too. After all
we're going to be partners, ain't we?

Billie

Sure, on the stage.

Roy

Sure. (*She starts up stairs—he follows.*) And
I know what's best for you. Just think of your
career—here you got the opportunity to hook up
with me in the act—we mustn't let nothing get in
the way. You got talent, kid, when I bring it out.
We're likely to be the sensation of vaudeville—
everybody talking about us. Why, I can see our
names in lights now—Roy Lane and Company.

(*Exits up stairs*)

(*The back door opens and* STEVE *enters quietly.
He holds door open and waits for* DOLPH.
*The latter is frightened. His hat has been
pushed to the back of his head. He walks
past* STEVE *and stands waiting.* STEVE *closes
the door—puts hat on piano*)

Steve

(*Nodding head toward cabaret*) You better go
in there for a while.

Dolph

What'll I do?

Steve

Why, get yourself something to eat, kid.

Dolph

You sure everything's all right?

Steve

(*Smiles, faintly scornful*) Ain't got any appetite, huh? (*Jovially*) You yellow bastard, I didn't think a little thing like that would bother you.

Dolph

Say, nothing bothers me if I know what's coming; but Jesus, I never seen nothing like this before.

Steve

That's why it's good. I've often thought it would be a nice thing if Scar was out of the way. And look at how it broke for us. Ever see anything prettier in your life? Now if Scar's mob has got any sense, I'll hook up the two gangs and run this town right—all the protection in the world, plenty of profits for everybody.

(PORKY *enters from down hall*)

Porky

Well, I got the Chicago boys out there.

Dolph

(*Jumps at voice*) Oh, that you, Porky?

Porky

All yelling for ring-side seats, so they can see the dimples.

Dolph

Well, I guess I'll have a drink.

(*Exits to hall.* PORKY *watches him puzzled.*

69

Turns and senses something eery in STEVE'S
over-deliberate lighting of a cigarette)

Porky

What's the matter, Steve?
(STEVE *blows out flame of lighter*)

Steve

Not a thing in the world, Porky.

Porky

You act kind of—

Steve

Kind a what?

Porky

I don't know.

Steve

Neither do I. (LIL *enters on stairs, carrying
props*) I'll go ask Nick if he knows.

Porky

(*Looking at* LIL) Well, I guess I'll stay out
here.

Steve

Go to it. (*Starts out*) Lil, have you met my
friend Mr. Thompson?

Lil

I don't know as I have—How are you?

Porky

Pleasure. (*Nods*)

70

Steve

Great admirer of yours. (*Exit to office*)

Porky

I've seen you before, Miss Rice.

Lil

That so?

Porky

Yes, from out in the audience—out in front, I guess they calls it. You might have noticed me last night after your last song—I was applauding and—

Lil

They was two of you.

Porky

I mean, you know, extra loud—and yelling too— I yelled bravo, bravo.

Lil

Was that what you yelled? If I'd known that, I'd a done an encore.

Porky

I hadn't been in to see Nick since you joined the troupe. Steve, that is Mr. Crandall,—my business associate—he's in here quite a lot—and I dropped in, and I thought your stuff was extremely good.

Lil

Well, I certainly am flattered, Mr. Thompson. Who the hell's been monkeying with my props?

Porky

Very interesting, the life back stage.

Lil

All depends on how you look at it. Of course it's nicer here than in the regular theatre cause here there's nobody can drop scenery on you—all we got to dodge is the stuff out front.

Porky

Well, I'm going to be out in front looking at you.

Lil

Don't look at me—just listen to me. I guess when that squab scenery comes out, you won't pay much attention to the old timers.

Porky

Whadda you mean, old timers—I'm an old timer myself. Me. I'm allus strong for the guy that's been somewhere and seen something.

Lil

That takes me in—I've seen a lot.

Porky

Here too.

(DOLPH *enters down hall*)

Lil

There's your boy friend. I'll take the elevator.

Porky

Well, Miss Rice, I'd like to see some more of you, sometime.

Lil

Stick around.

(*Exits upstairs.* DOLPH *opens office door and jerks his head to* STEVE *to come out*)

Porky

Hey, listen, there's a gal I could fall for. No skinny-legged, slat-sided baby pidgeons like you guys pick. Me, I like a dame that can sit in a Morris chair and fill it.

Dolph

Say, Porky, you know Dan McCorn?

Porky

I speak to him—I ain't never been arrested by him.

Dolph

Cut the comedy. He's out there. Keep an eye on him for a second till I come back, will you?

Porky

(*Impressed*) Sure. (*Exit down hall*)
(STEVE *comes from office*)

Dolph

There's a bull out there.

73

Steve

What of it?

Dolph

Maybe there's something up.

Steve

Go home and go to bed.

Dolph

There might be.

Steve

Do you know him?

Dolph

Sure. Dan McCorn.

Steve

(*Taking a little interest*) Homicide squad. What's he doing?

Dolph

Sitting there reading a newspaper.

Steve

(*Impressed*) That don't look so good. (Joe enters from hall and goes toward office. STEVE takes him by the arm) Joe.

Joe

Yes, sir.

Steve

Run upstairs and ask Miss Moore—Billie Moore —to step down here.

Joe

Sure, Mr. Crandall. (*Exits upstairs*)

74

Steve

You better go out and cool off.

Dolph

Don't think I'm shaky, but—

Steve

Go on now. Keep out of sight for a while. (JOE *appears at the head of the stairs*)

Joe

She ain't changed yet.

Steve

Tell her it's important. (JOE *disappears*)

Dolph

Listen, you better fix the hoofer too.

Steve

(*Impatient*) Keep away from him or you'll get me in trouble—I know how to handle this.

Dolph

Listen, you still got that rod on you—let me get rid of it.

Steve

Oh, for God's sake, don't have a panic. Who do you think I am, Johnnie the Dope? Should I have my pockets sewed up or something because there's a bull in the next room? (JOE *comes downstairs,*

75

followed by BILLIE *in costume for opening number*)
(*To* DOLPH) Beat it. (DOLPH *goes out down
hall.* JOE *goes up hall*)

Billie

I haven't quite dressed yet. (*She goes to prop
table*)

Steve

I won't keep you a minute. Just a little something I want to ask you. (*She comes to him, hooking her dress*) Listen, cute fella, I want to ask
you a favor.

Billie

Why, Mr. Crandall, of course—

Steve

'Tisn't so much. I want you to forget you saw
Dolph and me helping that drunken fellow out of
here a while ago.

Billie

What drunken fellow? Oh, I know—out there—
I remember.

Steve

Well, I want you to be a good kid and promise
to forget to remember.

Billie

All right.

Steve

You see, he's a big politician—if it got out it
might cause a lot of trouble—just thought I'd warn

76

you so that—you know—if you happened to talk you might get yourself in a bad jam.

Billie

Oh, I wouldn't say anything.

Steve

I can count on you then.

Billie

Positively.

Steve

Oh, by the way, here's something else I just happened to think of. (*Takes out handkerchief in which he had wrapped bracelet*) Guess what?

Billie

Why, Mr. Crandall—how should I know?

Steve

Birthday present for you.

Billie

But, Mr. Crandall, I had my birthday.

Steve

Be smart and have two of them.

Billie

Oh, Steve—Oh, I never saw anything—Oh, Mr. Crandall—why it's beautiful!

Steve

I'm glad you like it.

77

Billie

(*Without too much conviction*)   But I couldn't
take it.

Steve

Now, listen, don't give me any of that silly talk—
why, it's just a little trinket that doesn't amount
to anything.

(*Buzzer sounds and lights flash*)

Billie

Oh, my goodness, there's the opening.

(MAZIE *enters on stairs—with costume, followed
by* ROY *and* GIRLS—*all in costume*)

Mazie

Hey, kid, you forgot part of your props.

Billie

Oh, did I?   Thanks, Mazie.

Roy

Come on, girls, there's the opening.   Make it
snappy now.

Ann

(*Snatching cigarette from Grace*)   Gimme a
drag on that weed before you kill it.

Ruby

Say, Grace, you better remember what I told
you about cutting in front of me in this number.

Grace

I will.

Ruby

See that you do.

Mazie

Aw, tie it outside.

Ruby

Who's talking to you?

Roy

Get your places. (*Pulls* BILLIE *away from* STEVE) Every night a first night. They all paid for their seats. Heavy cover. We got to be good.

Nick

(*Coming in from office*) Now, girls, tonight some pep; and for God's sake, remember, smile at the men.

Ruby

Smile at 'em—it's all we can do to keep from laughing at 'em.

(*With a swell of music* ROY *and girls exeunt to cabaret. As each one reaches the door, she picks up the dance step and sings, changing her manner from boredom to pep. The music becomes faint as doors close*)

Nick

(*Sits*) According to my bookkeeping, I owe myself money—I don't know.

79

Steve

Well, I've heard that before; how much, Nick? (DAN MCCORN *enters from hall door. He is a man about thirty; matter of fact and rather well dressed*) Well, good old Dan McCorn.

Dan

Hello, Boys. (*He turns to look at poker machine. Nick has risen alarmed—*STEVE *motions him to sit*)

Nick

What you want in here?

Dan

Oh, just dropped in.

Steve

You're unusually sociable, ain't you?

Dan

Well, mebbe—I paid the rent today and two grocery bills—that always makes me feel good.

Nick

Grocery bills shouldn't worry you if you would listen.

Steve

A square dick, huh?

Dan

Figure it out yourself.

(JOE *comes from hall with two drinks—sees* MCCORN *and quickly exits*)

Dan

Well, Nick, how's business?

Nick

Can't complain.

Dan

How's your business, Steve?

Steve

So-so.

Dan

Extending your trade a little, ain't you?

Steve

How do you mean?

Dan

Kinda moving up town?

Steve

Where do you get that idea?

Dan

Oh, I hear everybody's troubles.

Nick

And they got a lot of 'em, I bet you.

Steve

(*Deliberately*) Say, Dan, you don't suppose for a minute—

Dan

That you can't peddle it where you please. No, I ain't sayin' that, only, ain't it likely to cause trouble?

Steve

Trouble?

Dan

That's a bad bunch up there. Some of 'em two-term men.

Nick

Some of them gorillas of Steve's ain't such a sweet bunch either.

Dan

That's what I say—that's why it looks like fireworks. (STEVE *glares at* NICK)

Nick

Wouldn't you think with all the trouble it is to get it—they wouldn't fight over who sells it?

Steve

Well, some people ain't never satisfied.

Dan

By the way, seen Scar Edwards lately?

Steve

(*With mild surprise—as though he hadn't quite caught the question*) Speaking to me——

Dan

Well, not exactly. Have you?

Steve

About two weeks ago I saw him—at the races.

Dan

Speaking to him?

Steve

Why not? I gave him a tip that paid 20 to 1.

Dan

Yeah? You didn't see him, then, when he was here tonight?

Nick

Huh?

Steve

Here? Who?

Dan

You didn't, Steve? Huh?

Steve

(*Long pause*) Your arm is swelling, Dan, what did you put in it?

Dan

Scar Edwards was here, wasn't he?

Steve

Listen, Dan, Scar Edwards and me are personal friends, but we don't do business together.

Dan

Maybe that's why he came.

Steve

Don't be silly.

Dan

I'm not.

Nick

He wouldn't come to my place.

83

Dan

Well, he was in this neighborhood anyway—that much I know, cause I saw him myself.

Steve

You saw him?   Where?

Dan

Under a blanket in a Westcott Express truck, just a block and a half from here—lying on his face with a slug in his back.

Nick

For God's sake.

Steve

So they got him, eh?   That's too bad—Scar wasn't a bad sort when you knew him.

Dan

I hope to tell you.

Steve

Well, that's a tough break—I'm sorry to hear it.

Dan

Now that I don't sound so silly—who pulled that off?

Steve

How the hell should I know?

Dan

Funny part of it is, he didn't have a rod on him.

Nick

You find him—

84

Dan

No, the Westcott driver found him, when he came out of the lunch room. I got there shortly after.

Steve

Can you imagine that driver?

Dan

Yeh, lucky thing he found him so soon, still warm when I got there—

Steve

(*Casually*) What time was it?

Dan

Must have been—say—twenty minutes or half-past ten.

Steve

Well, I've been here all evening, haven't I, Nick?

Dan

I didn't ask you for an alibi, but since you mention it—let's have it—who was with you?

Steve

(*Revealing just a flash of chagrin at his slip, he controls himself and speaks calmly*) Why, Porky Thompson, and Nick here part of the time; Billie Moore—one of the girls; most anybody could tell you, they all saw me.

(PORKY *comes in from hall*)

85

Porky

(*To* DAN, *surprised*) Oh, you're here—I was looking at the show and—yeah—how are you?

Dan

Thompson, what time were you here with Steve and Nick tonight?

Porky

(*Hesitatingly.* STEVE *signals with his hands*) I came in—about—five minutes after nine—(STEVE *signals again*) yes, sir—five minutes after ten.

(STEVE *walks away with satisfied expression*)

Dan

Why so positive?

Steve

(*Cutting in*) I happened to ask him for the correct time when he came in.

Dan

You didn't have a watch?

Steve

Sure. But I wanted to see if I was right.

Dan

When he told you—then you knew you were right —is that it?

Steve

(*Righteous indignation*) Where the hell do you get off to sweat me?

86

Porky

What's the matter—what's up?

Nick

Someone killed Scar Edwards.

Porky

(*Smiles*) Well, well — (*Sees* STEVE's *look —
changes mood*) Gee, that's too bad.

Dan

You guys ain't thinking of goin' in mourning,
are you?

    (ROY *and girls come back in line with swell of
music and faint applause*)

    (LIL *enters on stairs*)

Roy

Holy gee, but the orchestra put that number on
the fritz—a bunch of plumbers—they're off the
beat like a night watchman.

Lil

Why ain't you guys out there giving the kids a
hand?

Roy

All set, Lil? I'm going to announce you.

Lil

Anybody out there?

Roy

Not yet. They don't come in as a rule till just before my big number. (*Exit to cabaret. Heard announcing*) Miss Lillian Rice! (LIL *exits to cabaret as orchestra plays blues*)

(*The girls change into the other costumes which they have left on the prop table*)

Dan

Nice looking bunch, Nick.

Nick

You got your eyes open, eh, Dan? Would you like to know one of 'em?

Dan

That red-headed gal sort of appeals to me.

Steve

Don't introduce him to Billie. I'm taking no chances.

Billie

(*Hears her name*) What?

Steve

Don't have anything to do with these handsome cops.

Nick

(*Brings* PEARL *down*) Pearl, I want you to be nice to my old friend, Dan McCorn, here.

88

Pearl

How are you?

Dan

I was thinking I'd seen you somewhere before.

Pearl

That's an old one.

Dan

On the level. You used to be dancing at—the Golden Bowl, didn't you?

Pearl

No, sir; not me. (*She goes back to her dressing table*)

Dan

(*Shakes hands with Nick*) Well, boys, I guess there's nothing else I can talk about just now—sorry to have took so much of your time.

Steve

(*Comes over to shake*) Hell, Dan, glad to give you all the time we got—only wish I could help you. I know you got your job same as I got mine.

Nick

Sure, it's best everybody get along.

Dan

Well, so long.

Nick

So long, Dan.

89

Steve

Come again, Dan.

Dan

Sure.   (*Exits to cabaret*)

Steve

Porky, take a stroll out.   (PORKY *follows* DAN)

Ruby

(*Seeing bracelet*)   Hey, will you look at that?
(*All girls crowd around*)

Ann

Let's see.   Where'd you get it?

Ruby

Where d' you s'pose she got it?

Mazie

Oh, gee the Knickerbocker Ice Company.   Gee,
you got him going strong.

Roy

(*Enters from cabaret*)   Well, Boss, they're eating it up out there.

Ruby

Well, hoofer, I guess you'll be looking for a new
partner.

Roy

What?

Pearl

Oh, boy, when'd he give it to you?

Grace

Some rocks!

Roy

(*Pushes his way thru girls and looks at bracelet*)
What you got there?

Ann

Steve gave it to her.

Roy

You ain't gonna keep it?

Mazie

Certainly she is.

Roy

Give it back to him.

Billie

Now, Roy—

Roy

Listen, Billie, for God's sakes, don't be a fool!
You know what everybody'll be saying about you.

Billie

Don't tell me what to do!

Roy

I tell you give it back to him.

Billie

Listen, General Pershing.

Roy

You do what I say.

Billie

Mind your own business.

Roy

Please, Billie, I'm telling you something straight from the heart—

Nick

(*Pushing* BILLIE *out of the way*) Hey, hey, what you gonna do—have some heart talks instead of doing your number?

Roy

No, sir, Mr. Verdis. I'm right here waiting to do my stuff. Nobody can say I don't give the customers one hundred percent every performance. The night my old man died, I went out at the Regent Theatre in Danbury and give as good a performance as I ever done in my life. (*Turns and looks at* BILLIE) And even if a jane I'd put my hope and trust in was going to hell, I could still go out and give 'em my best. Line up, kids.

(PORKY *enters from hall*)

Porky

Dan McCorn is sittin' out there waitin'. What to hell's the matter?

Roy

There's the cue. Give it to 'em. Cut 'em deep

and let 'em bleed. Here we go. Here we go. Let's mop up.

> (*While the two men stand looking at each other inquiringly, the cabaret doors open, the music swells,* ROY *puts on a little hat with a feather in it, and dances out behind the girls*)

CURTAIN

ACT TWO

Half an hour later.

Music in cabaret.

PORKY sits picking his teeth—shakes his head pessimistically. He tosses a coin—is dissatisfied with the result.

STEVE enters from hall; closes the double doors.

Steve

Good thing I went out there and calmed down them Chicago gorillas. If they kept on talking shop so loud, I'd lost my reputation as a butter and egg man from Florida.

Porky

Dan McCorn still out there?

Steve

He's talking to one of the pick-ups.

Porky

Wish to God he'd go for good.

Steve

I don't know—he seems to be having a good time.

94

Porky

I seen 'em act that way before. Believe me, I
think he's getting all set to make a pinch.

Steve

Cut that out. Don't be so jumpy. What makes
you so jumpy every time somebody gets bumped
off?

Porky

Well, I was thinkin', maybe he's got a lot of
bulls hanging around the block for all we know.
(STEVE *lights a cigarette*) Say, Steve, tell me
on the square, you know who done it, don't you?

Steve

I haven't the faintest idea.

Porky

Well, you know it ain't healthy for you to hang
around here after Scar's been killed, don't you?

Steve

Are you talking to me?

Porky

Sure thing I am.

Steve

(*Stops him with look—then speaks casually*) A
gang shooting is no novelty in this burg. The cops
will be glad he's out of the deck.

Porky

(*Summoning up his courage*)   But, Steve; you done it, didn't you?

Steve

I don't know a thing about it.   Me and the deceased was great friends.   We'll spare no expense in giving him a swell funeral—flowers—all kinds; we'll make it the biggest event of all the season— a great success; and tell the boys I want 'em all to turn out for it.

Porky

Say, you talk like it was his wedding.

Steve

Not much different at that.

(*Knock on back door.   Pause*—STEVE *gestures to* PORKY.   PORKY, *fearful but obedient, peeks thru shutters*)

Porky

It's Dolph.   (*He unbolts door and* DOLPH *slips in*) What's the matter?

Steve

I thought I sent you out for air.

Dolph

(*Pulls tabloids out from under coat*)   The morning papers just came out.

Steve

Yeah?

Dolph

A lot of stuff about Scar Edwards' bump-off. (*They each take a paper*)

Porky

What's it say?

Steve

Let's see.

Porky

(*Reading*) Gang leader murdered. Story on Page 4.

Steve

Pictures and everything. Say, that's quick work, ain't it? Dan McCorn himself only knew it about two hours ago. Wonderful what they do nowadays. We should be very thankful for these modern inventions, boys—keeps us posted on the underworld.

Dolph

Believe me all that stuff ain't gonna be so good for somebody—all this talkin' and chewin' about it.

Porky

"Harlem Gang Leader's Body Found in Roaring Forties. Old Gang Feud Likely To Break Out."

Steve

Read to yourself—

Dolph

(*Tensely*) It says the cops have got some hot tips.

97

Steve

Sure they have. Here's the real dope though—
Now listen—this is good, see. (*Reads*) "It is
learned from confidential sources that the police
suspect one of Edwards' own gang who is said to
have nursed a grudge against his leader. An arrest
is expected within 24 hours."

Dolph

What do you know about that— (*He takes the
paper from* STEVE *and reads as it trembles in his
hands*)

Steve

Smart boys, them cops. Yes, sir. Porky, you
want to be very careful how you conduct yourself
in the future because them fellows don't let nothing
get by.

Dolph

It says they suspect one of Scar's own crowd, huh?

Steve

That's what it says. Well, that's my theory.
It's a good hunch, don't you think so, Dolph?

Dolph

(*Dumfounded*) Sure.

Porky

But even if the cops don't bother us—they's
something in that gang-war talk all right—

Steve

What do I care? I got you two boys to protect me.

Dolph

Listen, Steve, this ain't as sweet as it looks.

Porky

Dolph is right.

Steve

Oh, shut up. (*Quietly*) I certainly get a lot of coöperation out of you two. For the love of God pull yourselves together.

Porky

We're together.

Steve

Anybody'd think you was a couple of Staten Island hicks trying to find the Subways.

Dolph

Well, what's the matter? I was just tipping you what was going on—

Porky

He was just thinking about your safety, Steve. (DOLPH *crosses to door under stairs, peeks out*) Wish I knew who done it—I'm worried.

Steve

(*Steps toward* PORKY) Will you shut up or will I crown you with a gun butt?

99

Porky

I'm shut—(STEVE *strolls away*) But I'm worried just the same. What if the Edwards' outfit bump me off?

Dolph

Me too.

Steve

Well, what of it? You only have to die once. You got nothing to worry about—I'll bury you right—I may get a special professional rate from Campbell's if they get both of you. (*Laughs*) Say, quit worryin'. I wish they would start something. We'll go up to Harlem in a couple of fast cars and let these Chicago boys show off some of their machine gun stuff.

Dolph

No, Steve, on the dead, whyn't you go out of town till this blows over?

Steve

(*Sits*) I got something here that interests me.

Porky

Take her with you.

Dolph

I hate to see this chorus amitshure playing you for a sucker. Why don't you take her for a ride and then stop off at Little Ed's Roadhouse?

Porky

Sure; we might all get in trouble if you stay here.

Steve

Say, have you both lost all your sense? If I wanted to get myself accused of the murder of Scar Edwards, the surest way to do it would be to blow town. No, I'm staying here because I am innocent.

(The cabaret doors open. The music swells to a finale with a crash of cymbals. There is applause, and the girls in Hawaiian costume, and ROY, *enter. They go to the prop tables, in perfunctory fashion, and gather up their belongings.* KATIE *follows* PEARL, *hands her a note and stands waiting for an answer)*

That's intermission. You go out now and keep the visitors from coming back here, and don't be rubbering at McCorn—act unconcerned.

Porky

Sure.

Steve

You too, Dolph.

Pearl

(As she finishes reading note) Tell him I'll come as soon as I've changed.

*(*PORKY *and* DOLPH *go to cabaret)*

Steve

Billie, I've been waiting here for half an hour trying to get a word with you. (MAZIE, *seeing that* STEVE *wants to be alone with* BILLIE, *takes her props and costumes and goes upstairs and out with the others knowingly*) In fact ever since I was out in front looking at you and saw that something was missing. Didn't you like the bracelet?

Billie

Oh, of course I did—awfully—I thought it was lovely.

Steve

Then why don't you wear it?

Billie

Well—I—Mr. Crandall, I'll explain about it a little later when we've got time.

Steve

We've got time now. This is the intermission, isn't it?

Billie

Yes, but I—I mean—

Steve

(*Takes her hand*) No, really, I want to know. I'm proud of you, little fella—so I thought it would be nice for you to wear my bracelet—

Billie

I did wear it for a while.

Steve

If you don't like it, I'll take it back to Tiffany's and change it.

Billie

Oh, I'm just crazy about it.

Steve

Then why'd you take it off?

Billie

Well, Ruby began making some dirty cracks about it—and then I got wise to what it really meant—

Steve

What does it mean?

Billie

I guess you know.

Steve

No, tell me. I just thought it was a good looking bracelet and you were a good looking kid and the two of you looked awfully well together.

Billie

It's a slave bracelet, isn't it?

Steve

I guess that's what it's called.

Billie

That's what they said—and they said if a rich man gives you one and you wear it, then that's a sign that you belong to him.

Steve

(*Quietly*) I don't mind if they say that.

Billie

Well, I do.

Steve

(*More urgently*) You like me, don't you? I know you like me—I can tell—

Billie

Yes.

Steve

And I sure like you—and—I want to be able to do things for you and—

Billie

It isn't fair to you—that—I mean I can't take this bracelet off you because it wouldn't be fair.

Steve

Don't you think I'd treat you right?

Billie

I s'pose I shouldn't have let you take me out at all, Mr. Crandall, because I know it sounds silly, but I'm not that kind of a girl, that's all.

Steve

Maybe that's why I like you.

Billie

I know there's nothing wonderful about being the way I am—I mean being virtuous, I s'pose you call it—I know lots of the best-hearted girls in the world that aren't, so it isn't that; but I mean it isn't fair for me to keep your bracelet because that's the way I am.

Steve

Well, listen, baby, have I ever tried to pull any rough stuff?

Billie

No you haven't, and that's what I always say—

Steve

Then why haven't I got as much right to hang around you as some of these other yaps?

Billie

Well, you're married, of course and—

Steve

No, I'm not.

Billie

They said you was.

Steve

No, I'm divorced—I'm all right—I'm divorced twice. Just because you're here in the show, don't

think I regard you in a light way—no indeed—
I'm no fly-by-night—I'm a very sincere sort of person, baby, and I want you to understand how I
feel about you. I'm crazy about you. Honest, no
foolin'. (*Draws her to him a little;* Roy *enters
on stairs*) Don't listen to nobody but me, kiddie—
cause I'll treat you right—

Roy

Mazie wants to see you right away, Billie.

Billie

Oh, does she—all right—excuse me.
(*She goes up and out.* Roy *summons up his
courage and comes down stairs, trying to look
unconcerned.* Steve *stands grimly waiting for
him.*)

Steve

Say, listen, actor [Roy *stops*] did anyone ever
hit you right on the nose?

Roy

Yeh, once—come to think of it—twice. Why?

Steve

I was wondering if you'd like to have it happen
again.

Roy

What did I ever do to you?

Steve

(*Recovering his calm*) Nothing—you couldn't.
I was a sucker to get sore. Forget it. (*He exits
to cabaret*)

(MAZIE *and* BILLIE *enter at top stairs*)

Mazie

Hey, Oilcan, what is this?

Billie

She never said she wanted me at all. You had
no right to say that, Roy.

Roy

What I done was for the best—I had to get you
out of hearing so I could chase that twenty-five-cent
guy out of here.

Mazie

(*Coming down stairs*) Listen to what's yapping
about twenty-five-cent guys.

Roy

He ain't a fit companion for Billie and from now
on I'm making it my business to see that he don't
have nothing to do with her.

Mazie

Where's your wings?

Billie

(*Following them*) Well, Roy, it seems to me you're taking an awful lot for granted without consulting anybody.

Mazie

And picked out an exciting job for himself too.

Roy

In the first place, you ain't going to stay to his party tonight.

Mazie

She certainly is.

Roy

It's no place for a nice girl like Billie.

Mazie

Oh, I see. But it's perfectly all right for me though, eh?

Roy

Well, maybe you know how to handle gorillas— you know your goolash, she don't.

Mazie

Billie'll be all right. Steve's a fine fellow and he's just out for some innocent fun—

Roy

Says you—

Mazie

Says I—

108

Roy

This staying up all night running wild, drinking poison, don't get you a thing—I'm no prude, I'm for light wines and beer—but if a girl wants to get ahead in this racket, she shouldn't start out her career partying with rough-necks. In the second place—you're going to give back that bracelet.

Mazie

Give it back—ha! ha! Now I'll tell one. Why she could get five hundred for it in hock. Listen, Small Time, this little novice has got a great chance to grab off a millionaire if she works her points. Are you going to stand around and try to gum it?

Roy

I certainly am.

Mazie

Then you ain't the gentleman I thought you was. He might marry her. Did you see that cracked ice? When Steve gives up like that, he's gone, hook, line and sinker.

Roy

Marry!

Mazie

I'm telling you—hand embroidered nightgowns and everything—

Billie

Now, if you're all done discussing me, perhaps I could say a word myself.

Roy

Well, if there's any thought of his trying to get away with that marriage stuff, it's time for me to do something definite.

Mazie

Sure it is—bow yourself out of the picture.

Roy

Is that the way you feel about it, Billie?

Billie

No.

Roy

All right. Then I'd like to speak to you about something very private. (*To Mazie*) Would you kindly leave us?

Mazie

Go to it. I got to get in some work on a sandwich anyhow. Don't believe a word he says, Billie. (*Exit upstairs*)

Billie

(*Comes to him*) Roy, I wish you wouldn't keep acting that way.

Roy

What way is that?

Billie

Just going around arguing with everybody and making trouble.

Roy

I'm going to save you from getting into a lot of trouble.

Billie

I didn't ask you to.

Roy

I know you didn't. And take it from me, I ain't achin' to play the hero in this picture myself, but there's nothing else to do. Now first, I'm going to put a plain proposition to you. (*He comes toward her, half appealingly. She sits, looking up at him*) I guess you know pretty well that I'm very strong for you, but I ain't said nothing about matrimony on account of my old man has just recently died. But since this big four-flusher is talking about a wedding ring, I'll play my own ace. Listen, honey, how about getting hitched up?

Billie

(*Faintly*) Roy, I don't know.

Roy

It would be better for the act, wouldn't it?

Billie

I never thought much about it.

Roy

I s'pose I should of tipped you off how I felt before, but anyhow there it is in black and white.

Billie

(*Distressed*) Gee, I don't know what to say.

Roy

Take your time. I know it's kind of sudden. But I sort of thought you was wise to how I felt anyhow.

Billie

Well, I did think you liked me—I mean I hoped you liked me.

Roy

Well, now that you know how much I like you, what do you think about the idea?

Billie

(*Rise*) I don't know what to say.

Roy

I always thought, way down in our insides we knew we was for each other. God knows I'm for you, Billie girl, so just say the word that you're for me and I won't let out no yells or nothing, but I sure would feel just like doing that little thing. (*She doesn't answer*) What do you say?

Billie

Well, Roy, of course I'd have to think a thing like this over and—

Roy

Nothing doing. Just as easy to say it now as some other time.

Billie

How can I say it, when I don't know for sure whether I'm in love with you or not?

Roy

Well, we certainly get on well together.

Billie

Oh, I know we do, just wonderful.

Roy

Well, when you see me coming to say hello to you in the morning, don't your heart never beat no faster?

Billie

Yes, it does.

Roy

Well, that's it. That's what they call love at first sight, kid. It's wonderful. I'm the same way.

Billie

But I don't know if we ought to talk about marrying when we're so poor—

Roy

(*He comprehends her reason for hesitating*) Oh, (*Turns away from her, hurt and tense*) you want a rich guy—

Billie

I didn't say that.

113

Roy

(*Contemptuously*) A gold digger.

Billie

I'm not. I'm not. But I don't want to be foolish and say something that I'll be sorry for afterwards. All I say is that I ought to think about a
thing like this.

Roy

Aw, you want to think.

Billie

Yes.

Roy

All right, my duty's plain—Go on upstairs and
think.

Billie

Well, don't talk to me that way or I never will
marry you.

Roy

(*Dismissing her*) Sure. Talk it over with you
next week. (*She bites her lip to keep back the tears
and runs upstairs.* Roy *watches her until she's off,
then goes to phone and drops a nickel in slot*)
Hello—I want long distance. (*Gets returned nickel*)
Long distance? I want to get Trenton, New Jer-
sey. I want the Capitol Hotel there and I want
to speak to one of the Maloney Brothers. No, not
Baloney — Maloney — Maloney — M-a-l-o-n-e-y —

114

"M" as in matrimony. Yes, that's right. Maloney—
there's two of them in the act and anyone of them
will do. Make it snappy, girlie, will you, cause this
is a very important call. How much will this set
me back? What? Gee—well, all right. This is
Roy Lane, Circle 5440—now do me a favor, sister,
and put this call through right quick, will you,
please?

> (*During the latter part of his speech,* BILLIE
> *enters from dressing room and comes down-
> stairs hesitatingly*)

Billie

(*Pleadingly*) Roy— (ROY *hangs up*).

Roy

What do you want?

Billie

I ought to explain.

Roy

Now, listen, I told you where I stood. All you
got to do is say yes or no.

Billie

First you ought to give me a chance to explain.

Roy

(*Comes closer*) Hey, you've got your make-up
all streaked. You been crying.

Billie

Yes, I have.

Roy

One of the first things every artist should learn is, never cry during a performance.

Billie

I cried because of the way you talked to me.

Roy

Forget it, forget it. I'm wise now to how you feel—that's what I wanted to know. I got my duty, that's all.

Billie

But you don't know how I feel. You never gave me a chance—

Roy

I got the idea and just now I'm expecting a phone call, so—

Billie

You make me feel terrible. I don't want a rich man, but I know that it's just awful to be poor.

Roy

Well, tomorrow—

Billie

(*Almost in tears*) All my life everybody I've known has been poor and my mother always says, whatever you do, don't marry a poor fellow—

116

Roy

Well, for God's sake, haven't I told you what they get on the big time vaudeville and productions? (*Phone rings*) All right. Now get out of here, willya. This is a business call. (*She exits upstairs. Roy, at phone*) Hello—Yes, I'm trying to get Trenton. All right. (*Drops quarter in slot*) There you are, sister—Hello—hello—This one of the Maloney Brothers? Jack? Oh, Babe—Babe, this is Roy—How's the act going? Yeah. Got you opening the show, eh? Well, don't worry, Babe. I'll take a peek at it—I'll probably make some suggestions that will fix it O.K. That's duck soup for me, you know. What? Oh, nothing's wrong with me. Everything's O.K. But listen, Babe— (*Lights flash. Buzzer sounds. Ruby, Grace and Mazie in school girl costumes enter from dressing rooms, come down stairs talking*) Listen, can you hear me—I want you to do me a big favor—listen— Have you got a pencil? (*Continues talking— speaking low*)

Ruby

Sure, we'll have to stay for Steve's party. Who's yowling about it?

Grace

Oh, Billie.

(*Girls get school books and slates from prop table*)

Ruby

That one.   Guess one party won't spoil her.

Mazie

How many did it take to spoil you?

Ruby

You ought to know—I saw you at the first.
  (*They all wrangle at once*)

Roy

(*At phone—turns to them*)   Hey, take it easy.

Mazie

Steve's passed you up like a white chip, ain't he, dearie?

Ruby

Say, want me to haul off and knock you down?

Mazie

If you do, I'll bounce up and separate your ideas from your habits.

Grace

There's the cue.
  (*The three girls quickly form in line and exit
  to cabaret singing with baby voices, "M-i-s,
  s-i-s, s-i-p-p-i," etc.*)

Roy

(*At phone*) You're a life saver—do as much for you sometime, so long. (*To* PEARL *who appears on stairs in Pirate costume*) Want the phone?

Pearl

No, I gotta meet a John.

Roy

I got a John I'm going to meet pretty soon and bust him right square in the beak. (*Grabs hat and books*)

Pearl

Say, Roy.

Roy

Yeah?

Pearl

You been extra sweet to me since I been around here and let me tip you off to something. Don't monkey with the Crandall fellow. You might get hurt.

Roy

Him? I'll have him in Sing Sing before I get through. (*Runs to door to listen for cue, but finds he has plenty of time and comes back*) You know what I think he really is?

Pearl

What?

Roy

A bootlegger.

Pearl

(*With assumed surprise*) No? You don't say so. Wait and see. (*Exit to cabaret in posture of Professor, while girls' voices are heard singing "School Days"*)

(PEARL, *finding herself alone, goes to phone,
looks in her purse for change, drops coin
in slot*. DAN *enters from cabaret*)

Dan

Hello. (*She hangs up quickly—and turns, on her
guard*) You got my note all right, did you?

Pearl

Sure.

Dan

Was you going to telephone?

Pearl

No, nothing important.

Dan

Positive?

Pearl

Didn't I tell you? (*Waits, then adds, impatient
to be away from him*) I gotta get ready for my
number in a minute.

(*Starts toward stairs*)

Dan

(*Stopping her*) I won't keep you long. (*She
waits, her back to him*) Seen Scar Edwards lately?

Pearl

(*Turns*) What?

Dan

(*Ignoring her bluff*) Have you?

Pearl

What's the idea?

Dan

You know who I am?

Pearl

Sure, you're a cop.

Dan

Well I know who you are too.   You're the girl
I seen palling around with Scar Edwards when you
were dancing up in the Golden Bowl.

Pearl

You never saw me.

Dan

(*Turns her to face him*)   Oh—yes—I—did.
Didn't I?

Pearl

Well, that's no crime, is it?

Dan

Not exactly.   Why are you working down here?

Pearl

(*Dropping bravado*)   You ain't going to give me
away to Nick, are you?

Dan

Not a bit. What I'm asking you is for my own information, see?—it don't go any further. Are you on the outs with Scar?

Pearl

No, and if it's all the same, would you mind calling him Jim?

Dan

Excuse me. (*Looks at her steadily*) You're keeping tabs on this bunch for Scar?—I mean Jim —is that right?

Pearl

(*Appeals to him*) He didn't want to put somebody down here he couldn't absolutely trust for fear they'd double cross him—a lot of dirty skunks, they wouldn't stop at nothing.

Dan

But Jim Edwards trusts you, eh?

Pearl

Sure (*With a sudden burst of confidence*)—we're gonna be married as soon as he gets his final papers.

Dan

(*Walking away*) That's too bad.

Pearl

What is? (*Pause*) Has he done something you want him for?

Dan

No, I haven't a thing on him, lady.

Pearl

Well, tell me straight—has something happened? You act so kind of funny.

Dan

You gotta finish this show tonight? Sing and everything?

Pearl

Sure, I go on again.

Dan

Well, I won't take up any more of your time then, —I just wanted to know if you'd seen Edwards tonight.

Pearl

No, I ain't seen him since breakfast, but—(*Again decides to trust him*) I don't know why I shouldn't tell you—he told me he was coming down here tonight to have a show-down with Steve.

Dan

Oh, oh, he told you. . . . Well, I'll be going along about my business—Thanks, Mrs. Edwards.

Pearl

(*Pleased*) In three weeks.

Dan

You just keep this under your hat, won't you?

Pearl

Will I? If I want to get out of here with all my neck, I will.

(Roy *and three girls come dancing in singing "Hie, oh, the merry oh"*)

Dan

Pleased to have met you.

(*Strolls out cabaret arch, then turns to his left and goes down hall.* Pearl *is puzzled—depressed—tries to shake off her fear—walks to stairs and exits.* Roy *grabs up a prop*)

Roy

After this, a little more room, girls, when I make that side kick.

Grace

All right.

Ruby

In your hat (Roy *exits to cabaret, dancing; the girls start upstairs*) Which one of you tarts got on my slipper?

Mazie

These must be yours, dearie, they're miles too big for me.

(Girls *go upstairs to dressing room.* Nick *and* Porky *enter from hall*)

Porky

I can't look at that hoofer no longer—a different
suit but the same old dance.

(BILLIE *comes down stairs with telegraph
blank and goes left*)

Nick

It's the best I can do for the money   (*To Billie*)
Where you going?

Billie

I'll be back in time for my number.

Nick

That ain't what I asked you.

Billie

(*At cabaret door*)   I want to give this telegram
to the doorman to send my mother.   If I'm going to
stay to the party, I have to tell her.

(NICK *gestures to go ahead.* SHE *exits up
hall*)

Porky

Is that the one that Steve is nuts about?

Nick

(*Shrugs*)   Yeh, I don't know why—but that's it.
He says she's got best looking legs in New York——

(LIL *enters on stairs*)

Porky

Legs ain't all one size—some is lean—some is fat.

Lil

(*At foot of steps*) And how do you like 'em, Mr. Thompson?

(PORKY *is embarrassed*—NICK *exits to office*)

Porky

Me? If a woman's got sense, I never see her legs.

Lil

Ain't you a comfort. (*She puts mirror and make-up on piano*)

Porky

Well, my friends say they liked your act very well.

Lil

Yeah? Did you like it?

Porky

Sure I did. Didn't you see me out there?

Lil

Yeah—but I was a little bit discouraged when I looked down and seen you was asleep.

Porky

What? Oh, my God, lady—no. No, that's the way I get—you know—carried away—I shut my eyes when I'm terribly interested.

Lil

I guess you didn't shut your eyes when the weanies was out there.

Porky

No. I wasn't interested. They wasn't nothing worth listenin' to, so the least I could do was to look at 'em. But your singin' was—well, I can't express it—it's like I says to a friend of mine sittin' next to me—I says, "I consider that she's got one of the finest voices of her sex," I says.

Lil

Well, I'm generally in key.

Porky

Sure you are, and that's more than a lot of these opera singers can say too. Listen, I want you to tell me how you do that singin' some time—a long personal talk if you know what I mean. You're stayin' to Steve's party tonight, ain't you?

Lil

(*Smiles*) I will if you do.

Porky

Sure.

Lil

Only don't ask me to sing, cause I don't know a single dirty song—that is, not dirty enough for that bunch.

Porky

This ain't no singing party. That bunch all lost their voices asking for bail.

(*Buzzer*)

Lil

(*Starts out*) Well, there goes the whistle. I gotta step out now and hit a couple of high ones.

(ROY *enters from cabaret*)

Porky

I'm coming too.

Lil

Sit where I can see you.

Porky

Sure—I'll be right at your feet.

(LIL *exits to cabaret*, PORKY *hurries down the hall*)

(ROY *stands looking after them.* BILLIE *enters from hall. He turns away from her, goes to prop table and begins to undress.* BILLIE *starts upstairs, expecting him to speak, but when he doesn't, she pauses*)

Billie

All I've got to say is, if you always treated me like you have tonight, you'd make a terrible husband.

Roy

Oh, that's all you got to say, huh?

Billie

I should think that would be enough.

Roy

Not for me. (*She starts up*) Come here a minute!

Billie

If you have anything to say, you know where to find me.

Roy

I gotta make a quick change, you know that.

Billie

(*Comes to him*) What is it?

Roy

Was you out there taking a drink?

Billie

No.

Roy

I'm glad to hear that anyways.

Billie

I was sending a telegram to my mother.

Roy

(*Startled*) What?

Billie

You tried to boss me so much I just thought I'd find out if I had a mind of my own. So I just went

and telegraphed that I wouldn't be home tonight
cause I'm going to the party.

Roy

Well, I'm sorry you done that. (*Takes off
trousers*) Listen to me, kiddie, if it's just to spite
me you're doing this, why, I'll eat mud.

Billie

It's not only that—it's because I have an obligation.

Roy

(*Throws trousers over arm and goes to her*)
Listen, partner, I've been your pal anyhow, and I
got some right to talk to you. Who have you got
the greatest obligation to in this world, huh—a big
rounder like Steve Crandall, who's got no respect
for pure womanhood, or your poor old gray-haired
mother who's sitting at home alone waiting for you?

Billie

But she's not alone—my sister's with her.

Roy

Oh. (*In disgust he throws his trousers in corner
and picks up others*)

Billie

If you don't think I got enough character to be
decent at a party, you better look for somebody you
got confidence in.

(PORKY *enters from hall*)

Porky

Your shirt-tail's hanging out.

(*Exit to office*)

Roy

(*Paying no attention to him*) That ain't the life for you. (*Getting on trousers while he pleads earnestly*) You don't want to be pegged with them bags, do you? They think they're wiser than Almighty God, the guy that wrote the book,—but when they're hittin' the home stretch for Potter's Field, they'll be wiser still. For God's sake, think of all the plans we made, Billie. Don't be a dumb-bell.

Billie

I'm not.

Roy

You're giving a good imitation of one.

Billie

I'd go if for nothing else, just to show you good and proper that I don't belong to you.

Roy

If you did, I'd spank your bottom.

Billie

Oh, you would—would you?

Roy

You bet I would—and if I catch you inhaling any of that poison, I'll spank you before the whole mob.

Billie

Then I would be finished with you.

Roy

I don't care if you never spoke to me again. I gotta do my duty by my partner—first the artist, that's me—second, the human bein'. (*Buzzer*) *I* done everything I could to appeal to your better instincts. I pulled every wire I knowed to keep you decent and we ain't heard from all the precincts yet. (*Tries out comedy hat*) I told you just what my feelings for you is, nothing up the sleeve so far as I'm concerned, so if you want to be sore, I guess that's how it'll have to be, that's all.

(*Dances into cabaret in comic position*)

(PORKY *comes in from office—stops a second in door, talking into office*)

Porky

Sure you're right, sure you are. (PORKY *sees* BILLIE *who has started upstairs, shuts door and crosses to middle of the room*) Say, little girl, did you see . . . ? (*The party doors open and* DAN *appears*) Ah, yeah—well, never mind, I'll talk to you about it some other time.

(BILLIE *looks over railing to see who it is, then exits*)

Porky

Well, hello Dan. What you doin' in here? I thought you was out with one of the frails.

Dan

(*Coming down*) I'm broadminded. I go in for everything. Got a light?

Porky

(*Lights match*) Sure. (PORKY'S *hand shakes*)

Dan

What are you shaking about?

Porky

I'm not shaking.

Dan

(*Laughs*) Sure you are. Look. (*He holds* PORKY'S *wrist*)

Porky

That's the way I always get.

Dan

When a cop's around?

Porky

No, when I'm in love.

(DOLPH *enters from hall. Stops alarmed at seeing* PORKY *and* DAN *together—then hurries back down hall*)

133

Dan

Ever been accused of murder?

Porky

(*Inarticulate with fear*) Me? Listen, Dan, don't get me wrong—that stuff ain't in my line.

Dan

Oh, no, no—I didn't mean that—I was thinking about a fella I knew—it's tough, that's all—it's tough.

Porky

Oh, very tough.

Dan

This fella would a been all right if he'd told what he knew in the first place—but he tried to hold out.

Porky

Oh, gee, what a mistake—always come clean, that's me—always come clean.

Dan

He was mixed up with kind of a sour crowd and—

Porky

That's another thing: bad company; that's something we all should avoid. Eh, Dan, ain't I right? Listen, Dan, I didn't have nothing to do with this thing—I—

(STEVE *strides down hall, followed by* DOLPH *who hovers in the background*)

134

Steve

What the hell you trying to do, Mac, crab my party?

Dan

No, I'm waiting for someone who saw Scar Edwards when he was here.

Steve

Well, we've all told you he wasn't here?

Dan

You might be mistaken.

Steve

No one around here has got any reason for holding out on you. If I saw him, I'd say so—why not?

Dan

You might forget.

Steve

Bushwah.

Porky

I think some of his own crowd done it that got jealous.

Dan

I figger different. You see he didn't have a gun on him, and he was shot in the back, which looks to me like he come peaceful to have a showdown— and just for that one reason he didn't carry his cannon.

Porky

Well, I said once—and I'm willin' to repeat it—
I didn't know him.

Dan

(*Sharply*) How do you know you didn't see him
since you don't know him?

Porky

Well—I—there wasn't anyone here when I
came in.

Dan

(*Slowly*) No one?

Steve

(*Cutting in quickly, but keeping his manner deliberate*) Well, I was—but I was in the office.

Dan

(*Without looking around*) Oh, and you were
where, Dolph?

Dolph

I was out riding with a couple of janes—and if
you want me to bring 'em into court and tell about
it, I'll be glad to oblige you. (*Innocently*) Why?
What's happened?

Dan

No matter what it is, you got your alibi all fixed
now, eh?

Dolph

(*Advancing*) What do you mean?

Steve

(*Pulling him back*) Dan don't mean a thing,
Dolph. Treat him civil even if he is a dick.

Dan

When did you get here tonight, Dolph?

Dolph

Early, then I left Steve here and went out for
the ride.

Dan

You left Steve alone?

Steve

No, Porky was here.

Dan

(*To Dolph*) When you left?

Dolph

No, I was—

Porky

I was just coming in when he was going out.

Dan

(*Slowly*) Oh, now I got it—Steve was here when
Porky comes in, but Porky didn't see him cause
Steve was in the office— (*To* PORKY) Well, how
did you know Steve was in the office if you didn't
see him?

Porky

Why—

Steve

(*Stepping toward* DAN *belligerently*) He could hear me talking—the door was open. Say, for Christ's sake, Dan, you been all over this once. Now, listen, if you think any of us here had anything to do with it, why go ahead and make the pinch; let's get some bail fixed and get it over with. But for God's sake, don't stand around here and make a coroner's inquest out of the place. I got a party on here tonight.

Dan

Well, now listen, sweetheart, why get excited? You know it's my business to ask questions, ain't it? I know you guys didn't have anything to do with it, but I got to make a report and I'm workin' at this from a couple of angles.

Porky

Sure, Dan—that's right.

Dan

Trouble with you, Steve, is that you've had so much business with a lot of half-baked federal dicks you ain't used to talking to just a plain old New York cop any more.

Steve

(*Placated*) Well, maybe you're right.

138

Dan

I ain't always—I been wrong lots of times, but this case of Edwards interests me terribly. You see, whether a guy shoots square or not, according to the law, ain't always it—but no matter what he's done, to me, he should have a break; and somebody shot this guy in the back. (*Starts out*)

(BENNIE, *a thug in a dress suit, enters from hall*)

Bennie

Hey, fellows— (DAN *looks him over*)

Dan

Well, Bennie, you're out in Chicago now, eh?

Bennie

Huh? What's the idea? (DAN *exits down hall*)

Dolph

(*Between his teeth, going to hall door*) The son of a bitch.

Bennie

Who's that guy?

Porky

Dan McCorn.

Steve

What you doing back here, Bennie? We ain't ready for you yet.

Bennie

The boys want to be with the lingerie. (*Buzzer*)

The nerve of that big stiff looking at me that way!

> (GIRLS *start coming down stairs, dressed in Pirate costumes* — GRACE *crosses to piano, then* PEARL, *then* RUBY *and* MAZIE, BILLIE *and* ANN)

What's the idea anyhow?

Steve

Nothing that concerns you, Bennie.

Ruby

Ready, Pearl?

Pearl

Sure, I'm ready.

Steve

A local nuisance by the name of Scar Edwards got bumped off tonight, that's all.

> (PEARL *at the mention of Scar halts her descent. As the sentence is finished, she gives a scream, loses her grip on the stair rail and falls down the steps in a faint*)

Grace

What—what's the matter? My God.

Mazie

(*Hurrying to her*) Pearl.

Steve

What happened?

Ruby

What to hell happened—

Ann

What happened; what's the matter?

Billie

Pearl! But, dearie, you must of—

Pearl

I'm all right.

Mazie

What is it, Pearl?

Pearl

(*Trys to push them away*) I tell you I'm all right.

Mazie

Gee Christmas, kid—

Steve

What'd you do?

Pearl

I tripped on the stairs. That's all.

Ruby

I thought you fainted.

Pearl

Fainted? For what? Twisted my ankle, that's all.

(BILLIE *helps* PEARL)

Steve

Sure you're all right?

Pearl

Sure I am.

Mazie

(*Waving him away*) She'll be all right.

Steve

(*Turns back, dismissing the incident*) All right, Bennie, bring your bunch back—pretty near time anyhow—Go ahead, Dolph.

(*Exit* Dolph *and* Bennie *to hall*)

Come on, girls. I want to buy you a drink. What say?

Mazie

We can't now, Steve. We're on for this flash you know.

Steve

Well, I'll have a flock of them waiting for you as soon as you come off. All ready for a big night?

Mazie

Try us.

Steve

I'm going to. Now here you are, girls—see these $100 certificates? Well, you each get one of them.

(Pearl *sits at back, her head down;* Billie *stands aloof; the others crowd around*)

Girls

One for each?

Grace

Atta boy.

Mazie

You tell 'em.

Ann

Me for you.

Ruby

Go to it.

Steve

Wait a minute—this is the way we do it—I'll tear
'em in half and give each one of you your bit—now
if you're all good babies, when the party is over,
I'll tack the other half on.   Fair?

(*He tears the bills in half and starts passing
    one part to each of the girls*)

Mazie

Sure it's fair.

Grace

Three cheers for Steve.

Ann

This sure looks like a good start.

Ruby

Everything is hotzy-totzy.

Steve

Just be yourselves with these friends of mine
and the sky's the limit.   This party will be nobody's

143

business. Here, Pearl, if you make good you get the other half—

Pearl

Don't worry! I'll make good.

Steve

Atta baby. Here, Billie. (BILLIE *won't take hers* —STEVE *laughs*) I'll keep it for you.

(ROY *enters from cabaret*)

Roy

Come on, girls, give 'em your best. This is a short one. I just got a flash at a guy standin' in the back that I thought was Al Jolson.

Girls

(*Excited*) Oh!

Roy

On your toes—alley op.

(*They put daggers in mouths and slink into cabaret to sneaky music*)

Porky

(*Crossing to* STEVE) Did I say the right things?

Steve

What do you mean?

Porky

To Dan McCorn!

Steve

Sure, don't worry about him. Forget it——

Porky

I do, but——

> (Joe *opens doors of party room. It is now
> brightly lighted—the table set—the waiters
> hurrying about making final preparations*)

Steve

(*Calling to party room*) Joe, fix up some high-
balls and make mine a strong one.

> (Bennie *and* Dolph *come in from hall with
> Chicago mob.* Porky *does comedy lock-
> step.* Bennie *kicks* Porky *in fun*)

Come on in, boys—what do you think of it, huh?

Mike

Class, all right.

Steve

Nothing like this in the loop.

Larry

This is get-together week in old Manhattan.

Bennie

The place you got to go through to get to Chicago.

Dolph

Wait till you're here awhile.

Bennie

It looks like a big night.

Larry

How long before we meet the dames?

Steve

They'll be here in a minute. (*Cheers*) Now remember, boys, no shop-talk to-night—everybody here don't know our racket.

Dolph

Steve, you better be the one to serve out the introductions.

Porky

And don't let anyone sing the prisoner's song or we'll all be in tears.

(*They laugh*)

Dolph

Here they come, come on boys, step up, don't be bashful.

(Girls *come rushing in from cabaret*)

Steve

Here we are—now how about the drinks?

Mazie

Not yet, Steve, this is the quick change for the finale.

Ruby

The parade of the nations.

146

Dolph

Step up, fellows. Don't be bashful.

(*The* CHICAGO MOB *get an eye-full.* GIRLS *keep right on with their change. They now change to Flag Costume*)

Steve

Let me present you, fellas. Boys, this is Miss Billie Moore—and this is Mazie.

Mazie

Just Mazie? I got another name.

Steve

Excuse me—Miss Mazie Smyth.

Mazie

Smith—ordinary Smith.

Steve

Excuse me again—common ordinary Smith.

Mazie

Ordinary, but not common.

(*All laugh*)

Steve

And here's Ruby—Pearl—Grace.

(*To* ANN)

What's your name, Baby?

Ann

(*Weakly*) Ann.

(*All laugh*)

147

Steve

Sure—Ann it be.

Larry

Glad to be wid youse.

Steve

Girls, my friends from Chicago.

Ruby

My Gawd, from way out there in Montana?

Larry

Illinois.

Porky

She's kiddin'.

(NICK *enters from office*)

Steve

And here's the old chief himself. Boys, this is Nick Verdis, a regular—he's paid so many fines, he owns stock in the White House.

Larry

Glad to get in wid youse.

Bennie

Ya got some swell frills—yes, sir.

Dolph

I could use one right now.

Larry

Split one with you.

Duke

(*Shaking hands with* NICK) I heard of you, fella.

Nick

Any friends of Steve's is K. O. with me. Come on in here, and we can sit down.

(*Some of the men mingle with the girls and begin to get intimate*)

Bennie

Sit down and leave all this lingerie, am I crazy?

Steve

They got to finish the show yet—we'll see 'em all afterwards.

Mazie

(*Getting position*) Well, I hope to tell you.

Dolph

Me for you.

Mazie

Be generous—your friends may like me.

Roy

(*Rushes in from cabaret out of breath*) Ready to unravel the last one, kids?

(*The girls start parading out four steps apart, very regally*)

Steve

And, fellows, this is Roy Lane, better known as Personality——

Roy

(*Making change to Uncle Sam costume*) In person—not a moving picture.

Steve

Possibly the greatest living song and dance artist who never played the Palace.

(CROWD *laugh*)

Roy

There's a lot of time, Wisenheimer. I ain't worryin' about my future.

(*He follows girls into cabaret*)

Nick

Don't get him started now.

Steve

He's a character. I'm going to have him stay for a little while. He'll hand you a million laughs——

Nick

Come on, Chicagoes, I'll buy the first one.

(NICK *leads way to party room*)

Larry

We ain't exactly what you call broke ourselves, you know.

(*They all laugh and start drinking.* LIL *enters from cabaret*)

Porky

Wait a minute, gang. Here's one you ain't met yet. This is Lil, the silver toned song bird——

Lil

(*Kidding*)   Give the little girl a big hand.

Porky

Maybe we can get her to wobble something——

Dolph

How about silver treads amongst the gold.

Bennie

Nix—Nix——

Porky

One of these guys knows you, Lil—says he heard you sing at Jim Tomasso's joint in Chicago seven years ago.

Bennie

(*Yells*)   I said seventeen years ago.

Lil

What do you mean?   That was my mother.

(*Everyone laughs.*   DOLPH *hands* LIL *a drink. The* CHICAGO MOB *kid* PORKY *and* STEVE *ad lib while drinking and eating. The* GIRLS *and* ROY *enter from cabaret. There is substantial applause*)

Mazie

Well, that's over.

Grace

Now for the big feed.

Ruby

And, my Gawd, how I could use a drink!

Mazie

One of them guys is kinda good lookin'.

Ruby

What great eyesight you got.

Ann

She saw his pocketbook.

Mazie

Oh, you're waking up too.

Dolph

(*Steps out*) Come on, girls—let's have fun. In here everybody—— (PEARL *sits down overcome for the moment.* ROY *has started upstairs carrying his costumes and props*) Hey, young fellow, have a drink.

Roy

No, thanks, I just had my hair cut.

    (*He exits upstairs—the piano in party room is heard*)

Nick

(*To* PEARL) What's the matter with you?

Pearl

(*Recovering herself—tough*)   I'm waiting for someone to bring me a drink.

(BENNIE *and* LARRY *rush for* PEARL)

Larry

I saw you first, redhead.

(*Carries her into room*)

Porky

This way, everybody—— We'll get Lil to sing.

(*General hilarity*)

Nick

(*Switches off lights*)   Not so much noise——

(*He exits to hall.* BENNIE *chases* BILLIE *from party room*)

Bennie

Come on, jazz it up, blue eyes.

(BILLIE *frightened, runs toward* STEVE.   STEVE *grabs* BENNIE *toughly and throws him back into party room*)

Steve

Get to hell in there——

(DOLPH *closes the party room doors, leaving* BILLIE *alone with* STEVE. *We hear the piano dimly.* BILLIE *rushes to* STEVE *for protection*)

153

Steve

It's all right, Billie, don't be scared. Everything's all right.

Billie

Oh, Steve, what'll I do?

Steve

(*Holding her*) I won't let anybody bother you—— (*He looks at her tenderly—is suddenly overcome by his passion*) I love you—kid. (*Crushes her to him*) God, I love you. I'd do murder for you.

(*He kisses her passionately—— She tries to break away*)

Billie

(*Frees herself and goes to chair*) Steve, please don't.

Steve

All right—I'm sorry. (*Kneels beside her—contrite*) Listen, Billie, just to show you that I appreciate what a real nice girl you are, you don't need to stay to the party. You can go home if you'd be happier about it.

Billie

No, I ought to stay because I owe that much to you, and anyhow—— (*Looking upstairs after* Roy) I said I'd stay and I'm going to.

Steve

But you're such a little peach I want to make you happy—see. Listen, tomorrow night after the show let's get in the car—go for a ride and have a good talk. Will you? (*Nods*) All right, that's a date. We'll stop at Ed's place and get a nice little supper and I've got something important to tell you.

(*He starts to fondle her*)

Billie

Make your hands behave, Steve.

Steve

(*Drawing back*) All right, I'm just as meek as a lamb, see! Whatever you say.

(*The party room door opens and* MAZIE *chases* RUBY *out—others follow with great clamor*)

Mazie

I'll make your shirt roll up your back like a window shade.

Ruby

(*Drunk*) I'll step on you. I'll spit in your eye——

Dolph

Cut it out—— (*Separates them*)

(NICK *enters from cabaret*)

Nick

Hey, hey. Quiet. Quiet. Shut up that noise.

Mazie

No phoney blond with store teeth can pull that on me and live.

Nick

Shut it. Shut it. Take 'em back.

Steve

All right. I'll handle this.

Lil

(*To* PORKY) Andrew, dance for mama.
  (PORKY *dances Charleston. Fight breaks up, as couples begin to dance*)

Steve

Inside. It's all right, Nick. I'll pay for the noise too, so keep your shirt on.

Grace

Where's my boy friend?

Nick

(*To* STEVE) McCorn is sitting just outside there.
  (STEVE *herds them back*)

Steve

Listen, folks, the party is on the inside. Nobody is to come out here without a permit from the Chief—that's me.

  (ANN *leaps at* STEVE *winding her legs and arms about him; he carries her into party room*)

156

Ann

Hail the chief.

> (*Cheer from Party.* JOE *enters from cabaret with more drinks*)

Joe

I never seen such a thirsty gang.

Steve

Excuse me a minute, Billie.

> (*He shuts door to party room leaving only the two girls and* NICK *outside*)

Nick

(*Going*) What do they think this is, Ike Blooms?
> (*Exit to hall*)

Mazie

(*Going to* BILLIE) Ain't you having a good time?

Billie

I'm all right.

Mazie

Come on, have some fun—you're only going to live once.

Billie

You go ahead—don't pay any attention to me.

Mazie

Don't be afraid. Nothing'll happen to you. Listen, Billie, crack wise. It ain't so serious. Just kid 'em along, that's all, kid 'em along. It ain't so bad as it looks. I wouldn't give you a bum steer, kid, honest, I wouldn't—but you don't always want to pay too much attention to what people say. Take me, for instance, you think I'm a pretty tough character—sure I am, in a way,— but I seldom give up—very seldom——

(KATIE *enters from hall*)

Katie

Say, Miss Moore, here's a telegram for you.

Billie

(*Taking it*)   Me?

Katie

The hostess told me to bring it in.

Billie

Thanks.

Katie

'Sall right.

   (*Exit to cabaret*)

Billie

(*To* MAZIE)   Gee whiz, I'm scared of telegrams. Ain't it crazy?

Mazie

Once I got an offer of a job that way.

Billie

Yeah?

Mazie

Sure.   And it can't talk so you gotta read it.
(BILLIE *tears it open—reads—looks at* MAZIE *terrified*)   What's the matter, kid?   It ain't bad news?
(BILLIE *nods, bites her lip and begins to weep*)
What is it?

Billie

(*Passes her the wire, trying not to sob*)   It's
mamma.

Mazie

(*Reads*)   Mother very low—come at once.   Mary.

Billie

(*Rises*)   Oh Mazie, and to think I'm acting like
this and she's maybe dying.

Mazie

Now, Billie, maybe it ain't nothing at all—now
you get hold of yourself, Billie.   (ROY *enters on
stairs in street clothes*)   Roy, Billie's got some bad
news.

Roy

What is it?

Mazie

Her mother.

Billie

(*Going to him impulsively*)   Oh, Roy—she must
of had a stroke or something.   She was all right last
week—a telegram from Mary—maybe she's dying.
Oh, dear, oh how could I have acted this way.

Mazie

You didn't do anything, darling.

(*Pulls* BILLIE *from* ROY *and puts her arms about her*)

Roy

(*Pulls her right back into his arms*) It's all right, kid. Everything's all right now. You're among friends. We'll take care of you. (*She weeps more uncontrollably*) There. There.

Mazie

Gee, I can't stand seein' her like that.

Roy

It'll come out all right. Take it from me. Everything's goin' to be all right, Billie.

Billie

I want to go home.

Roy

Of course you do, and I'm right here to take you, too, honey. The sooner the better, so stop your crying now. Just leave it to me. Come on, let's get out of here fast.

Billie

You're so good to me.

Roy

You bet I'm good to you. Why wouldn't I be? Ain't we pals through thick and thin, that's us, kid.

Now you hurry and jump into your traps, honey, and we'll be on the train for Trenton in twenty-five minutes.

(STEVE *enters from party room. Inside they are singing and dancing*)

Mazie

Oh, Steve, Billie's got to go home—her mother's sick.

(*Hands him wire*)

Billie

(*To* STEVE) I'm awfully sorry. Mazie, have you got a handkerchief?

(MAZIE *shakes her head, calling attention to her undress.* ROY *dries her eyes with his*)

Steve

Well, that's tough luck but we'll see what we can do. To hell with the party. I gotta get you home. Hurry up now, the car's out back. I'll have you out there in no time.

(KATIE *enters from hall*)

Roy

You don't need to bother, Mr. Crandall, everything is already arranged, see?

Katie

Here's another one, Miss Moore.

Billie

What?

(STEVE *takes it and opens it*)

Katie

Almost like an opening night, or something.

(*Exits to cabaret*)

Steve

(*Reads to himself, then grunts*) Huh.

Billie

What's it say? She's not—?

Steve

(*Reads*) Your wire received. Stay to party and have good time. Mother.

(*They all look at each other*)

Roy

She must a got better.

Mazie

Ain't that peculiar?

Billie

I don't see.

Roy

Sometimes those things gets mixed.

Mazie

I'll say they do.

Steve

Well, everything's all right anyhow, isn't it? See?
All that worry for nothing. So dry up those tears
and powder the little nose and join the bunch.

Roy

I think as long as we planned to go, Billie, the
best thing would be to start out now and see for
sure if everything's all right. I'll take you home.
   (*He pulls her by one arm,* STEVE *holds her by
      the other*)

Steve

Of course she ain't going home.

Roy

It seems to me, it's the wisest thing to do.

Steve

(*Takes her with him*) No, she's going to stay.
Come along, Billie. You come on too, Lane. Do
your clowning.

Roy

I'm particular what kind of society I'm seen with.

Steve

Wait a minute.
   (NICK *enters hall*)

Roy

I don't know as I will.

163

Steve

What do you mean?

Roy

I mean Billie ought to get out of here—and as for me, I wouldn't stay and entertain your gang of goofers if you kissed my foot in Macy's window at high noon.

Steve

Why, you dancing tramp.

Roy

I know all about you. It's guys like you give New York a bad name.

Steve

You waxed floor bum.

Nick

Steve, easy. You want people out there to hear?

Steve

(*Controlling himself*) Tell him to get.

Nick

Get!

Mazie

(*Grabs* STEVE, *looking at telegrams*) Say, I just thought of something. This last wire is an answer to Billie's. Now, the other one is an answer to something else. I'll bet my winter underwear the boy-scout framed it himself.

164

Roy

You're full of chestnuts.

Steve

What?

Nick

Framed what?

Mazie

He was telephoning long distance. Billie, you told me yourself.

Roy

Maloney Bros., that's all.

(DOLPH *opens the party doors looking for* STEVE; *he senses something wrong and waits —others join him*)

Mazie .

He got the Maloney Brothers to send the wire.

Billie

Roy, you didn't?

Roy

Certainly I didn't.

Mazie

You certainly did.

Steve

So you framed a wire on her? That's the kind of tricks you're up to, eh?

Billie

Roy, you wouldn't scare me like that——

Roy

Don't pay any attention to any of 'em. (*Wavering*) Anything I done, I guess I'd know if I done it.

Billie

(*Seeing the truth in his eyes*) You did. (*Wounded beyond expression*) That's the dirtiest trick anybody could ever do. Oh, Roy, making me think——

(*Turns away*)

Roy

Now, Billie, listen——

Billie

I don't want to listen—I don't want anything to do with you—— You big sap.

Roy

(*Almost ready to cry*) Suppose I did do it. I did it for you, didn't I? I know these kind of guys and you can't be right if you run with guys like Steve Crandall—he's just out to grab you—and he don't care what means he uses—I'm tellin' you he's just plain no good and I don't give a damn who knows it.

(*There is a growl from the men. They move toward* Roy *threateningly, but* STEVE *stops them*)

Dolph

Hey, wait a minute.

Porky

What'll we do to him?

Ruby

What do you think of that?

Mazie

You're going fine——

Grace

Look who's here.

(STEVE *gives* PORKY *a quick instruction and
stands waiting for the girls to be taken out*)

Nick

No more. Nobody. Get back in the room.
There's still peoples out there.

Porky

(*Downstage*) Come on, girls, I want to tell you
a bed-time story. Come on now. All the girls in
with me. Come on, Billie.

(*Exits with girls and* PORKY *to party room—
he shuts doors*)

Steve

Now, you louzy little bum, I got you where I
want you.

(*Hits him and knocks him down*)

Roy

Thanks. (*Getting up*) Ain't you a brave guy
though—all right—look out for this one.

(ROY *rushes at* STEVE. STEVE *pulls his gun*)

167

Steve

And look out for this one.

Dolph

Don't shoot.   They'll hear you.

Joe

Cheese it.

Dolph

Look out, the dick.

   (DOLPH *grabs his arm, twisting his wrist.   In
      the struggle the gun is dropped.   Before it
      can be recovered, they become aware that
      DAN MCCORN has come in from cabaret.
      They are frozen into quiet.   ROY picks up
      the pistol defensively, without realizing that
      he has it*)

Dan

What's the matter, boys?

Steve

Little argument, that's all.

Dan

Little argument?   (*Goes to* ROY)   So little you
pull this?

   (*Snatches gun from* ROY)

Roy

That ain't mine.

Dan

No?   Whose is it then?

168

Steve

It's his all right—he pulled it on me just now.

Roy

You big liar.

Nick

Liar yourself, Lane. We all saw you do it.
(NICK *closes cabaret doors*—JOE *stands guard at party doors*)

Gang

Yes! sure!—we saw him.

Dan

(*To* ROY) You got a permit to carry this?

Roy

No, of course not——

Dan

Oh you're the boy that——

Roy

I'm the chief performer here, Mister, Roy Lane.

Dan

Oh, yes.

Roy

Singing and dancing specialties; this is just a filler-in.

Dan

Ever hear of the Sullivan Act?

169

Roy

What time is it playing?

Dan

The Sullivan Act is a law—it gives you plenty of time for carrying one of these.

Larry

You said it!

(*The gang laughs*)

Roy

I tell you it ain't mine.

Dan

No? Then I'll keep it till I find out who owns it. You better come along with me now.

(*Pulls* Roy. *Puts gun in his pocket*)

Dolph

(*Aside to* Steve) He's just stallin' about the hoofer. He wants the gun.

Steve

Shut up.

Larry

Who the hell is this guy, Steve?

Steve

He's a dick.

Bennie

The one I was telling you about.

170

Larry

Well, what the hell——

Bennie

What's the idea hornin' in—what's the idea——

Steve

Give him back his rod, Dan—I can settle my own arguments with him.

Larry

I'll say we can——

Dolph

You tell him.

Bennie

You bet you can.

Dan

So these are your friends from Chicago?

Steve

Listen, Mac, what the hell are you tryin' to do? You been gumshoeing around here all night. For what? Now you come buttin' in here around my party. Understand, *mine!*—— You ain't got a warrant to go tearing around here as you like. This room is private. Now I'll thank you to run along and call it a day—and give the kid back his cap pistol. I can settle my own arguments with him.

(DAN *stands surrounded*)

Dan

I said I'd keep the gun.

Duke

You said what?

Bennie

Not if Steve says to give it back—you won't.

Dolph

Yeah—you bet you won't.

Larry

Not while we're here.

Steve

Better give it up, Dan, while you're able and take the ozone.

Dan

(*Sees he's in tight place—changes his tone*) Well, Steve, you're a damn fine ungrateful guy for the finish—I'll say that. So I been gumshoeing around here all night, have I?

Steve

I'll say you have.

Dan

Shall I tell you why? You know Scar Edwards was bumped off tonight. You know the minute his mob heard it, they got together, didn't they? And where would they head for? Right here. And who would they be looking for? Why, for you. So I phoned over to the house and gets seven of the

boys to lay around outside in case that mob of
Scar's show up.

(STEVE *relaxes his aggressive pose a bit, and
the others follow suit*)

Steve

You did? You did that, Dan?

Dan

Just to protect you. There's three of my men
wasting good time out there in back now.

Steve

Dan, I didn't know that.

Dan

Besides maybe I saved you from getting shot up
by this Indian. (*Indicates* ROY) And you yelling
your head off about me buttin' in.

Steve

But you been hanging around all night asking
questions and acting like you really thought I might
have had something to do with Scar's bump-off.

Dan

Well, I gotta ask questions, Steve, but that don't
say I suspect you.

Roy

Well, I suspect him.

Nick

Oh, shut him up.

Roy

And I got a good reason too.   (*Points to* DOLPH)
I saw this guy and Steve helping a fellow with a
scar on his face out the back door there tonight.

Dolph

Who, me?

Steve

(*Starts for* ROY)   You're a liar.

Dan

(*Holds arm up—keeps* STEVE *from getting to*
ROY)   Wait! Wait a minute, Steve. Take it easy.
(*Pause—— To* ROY)   What time did you see Steve
with Scar?

Roy

Before the show—about 10 o'clock.

Steve

He's lying, Dan.

Dolph

Sure he is.

Dan

(*To* ROY)   Would you know this guy with the
scar if you saw him again?

Roy

Sure I would. I saw them and Billie Moore saw
them too. They were taking him out that door.
I asked, "Who's the drunk?" and Steve said, "One
of the boys we're helping home." If you don't be-

lieve me, ask Billie—she'd never tell nothing but the truth—ask her.

Steve
Dan, this kid is sore at me—he's jealous—he made up that rotten lie to get me in bad.

Dolph
Sure. Dan can see through him.

Dan
Verdis, call in the Moore girl.

(NICK *glances at* STEVE. STEVE *makes sign, so* NICK *goes up, opens party door*)

Dolph
(*During above, speaks to* DAN *confidentially*) Don't believe nothin' this hoofer says. I tell you, he's nuts.

Dan
(*Impressed*) Yeah?

Nick
Billie—hey, Billie—come—want to see you a minute.

Dolph
Sure—ask anybody—he's an awful liar.

(BILLIE *comes in. The other girls struggle after her curious*)

Billie
What do you want me for?

Grace

What's the matter?

Mazie

Why ain't you guys paying us attention——

Ruby

Shut up, look what's going on.

Dan

Miss Moore, (*The room becomes quiet*) Miss Moore, about 10 o'clock tonight, before the show started, when you came down to rehearse with the dancer here, did you see Steve and this gentleman (*Points to* DOLPH) helping a drunken man out the back door?

Billie

(*Unable to grasp the situation*) Why——

Roy

Tell the truth, Billie.

Dan

Did you? A man with a scar on his face?

(STEVE *turns and looks at her—she catches his eye—turns back to* DAN—*pause*)

Billie

No.

(STEVE *shrugs, satisfied, as though to say, "I told you"*)

Dolph

I told you that kid was nuts.

Dan

(*To* GIRLS) Did any of you see Scar here to-night?

Girls

No.

(PEARL *steps forward, starts to speak, then walks toward stairs*)

Ann

Who? Somebody else coming?

Nick

I'm here all the time. I didn't see him.

Steve

Now are you satisfied?

Dan

Yes.

Mazie

Say, copper, will you do me a favor? Take Personality with you before he tries to make any more trouble here.

Steve

Is that all you want, Dan?

Dan

That's all for now. (*Pulls* ROY *by the arm*) Come on, Lane. I'll tell you some more about the Sullivan Act.

Roy

You can't take me like this, officer—— Who's going to look after Billie? She don't know what kind he is——

(*The crowd starts back toward party room*)

Dan

Come on——

Roy

(*Desperately*) No. Wait a minute—— For God's sake give me a chance. She's only a kid. She don't know what she's up against. Mazie, tell him. This Crandall guy is out to grab her——

Steve

Take him along.

Roy

I'll fix you. (*Breaks away. Makes a rush at* STEVE—*is stopped by* BENNIE) I'll kill you if you touch her—— I will, God damn you. (DAN *recaptures him; yanks him toward back door*) Lil —somebody—why don't you say something! I don't care what you do to me—— Oh God, Billie.

(*The music starts up.* DAN *is dragging* ROY *out*)

CURTAIN

ACT THREE

In the cabaret the orchestra is just finishing the
    Battle number.   Joe sits on a chair, center,
    asleep.

Dolph comes down back and looks around—sees Joe.

Dolph

(*Growling to himself*) Hey! (*Kicks* JOE *on the
sole of the foot waking him with a start*)   What's the
idea?

Joe

I'm resting.

    (NICK *enters on stairs*)

Nick

What's the matter?

Dolph

I come in here and find this guy asleep.

Joe

The show didn't start yet.

Nick

That's enough, Joe.

    (JOE *exits muttering*)

Dolph

Now, listen, Nick, I gotta get out of here fast.

Steve phoned me to drop in and tell you that the stuff will be here at 3 o'clock.

Nick

What's the rush? I wasn't expecting it tonight. Where is Steve anyway?

Dolph

I don't know where he is just now, Nick. He might be going out of town for a couple of days. He phoned me to tell you about the truck.

Nick

Some trouble come up?

Dolph

No, no, everything's all right.

Nick

Listen, Dolph, you shouldn't hold out on me. Now, tell me straight what is it? If Steve is in trouble, then I should be the one to know as much as anybody——

Dolph

Everything is all right, Nick—everything is perfectly all right.

Nick

That hoofer done some pretty wild talking last night—and——

Dolph

Hey, don't pay no attention to him. He was sore at Steve, that's all—even McCorn could see that.

Nick

Yeh, but he might tell a lot of lies. They got him in jail—and——

Dolph

No, they ain't.

Nick

No?

Dolph

They turned him loose. They gave him the air a couple of hours ago.

Nick

Yeh?

Dolph

Sure—they could see he didn't have no sense— he was just a false alarm, so they threw him out.

Nick

Then why don't he come back to work? I gotta give a show tonight. Half my actors didn't turn up.

Dolph

I don't know anything about that. I just wanted to tell you about the truck, that's all. (RUBY *appears on stairs in kimona*) Hello, Baby, well, Nick —three bells it is, remember. So long. (*Starts for door and exits to hall*)

Ruby

Got any news yet? (*He looks up—shrugs shoulders*) Well, what d'you say? (*She comes down and sits*) Looks like we get a night off then—huh?

Nick

(*Looks at watch*)   Where the hell do you think
they is?

Ruby

Sleeping it off.

(JOE *enters from up hall with a slip of paper*)

Joe

(*Apathetically*)   Want to O.K. this?

Nick

Don't bother me.   (JOE *leans against the door
and waits—bored*)   Got to think someways to give
some kind a show tonight: Pearl not here, Billie
not here, Lil not here, the hoofer not here—every
other time he's around so much I don't want to see
the sight of him—tonight when I need him, where
is he?   Go on, let me alone.

(JOE *exits to hall again*)

Ruby

Steve's party sure busted up the show for fair.
That Chicago spendthrift I drew must've been born
in Scotland.   (ROY *enters back door in street
clothes*)   Here's God's little gift to the night clubs
now.

(NICK *looks at him, waiting for explanation.
ROY ignores him—walks to the prop table
and begins to collect his belongings*)

182

Nick

Jesus whiz, you're late.

Roy

Late for what?

Nick

For work.

Roy

Ease off, Greek, you didn't think I came back to this bucket of blood to work, did you?

Nick

Why not?

Roy

After what you slipped me last night?

Nick

I don't know what you're talking about.

Roy

You thought we parted good friends, did you?

Nick

Oh, a little thing like that—we forget—it's just like I says to Steve last night—I says, don't be mad at the hoofer, he can't help it—he's just a little nutty. Now here it is pretty near time for show to go on—I need you, you need me——

Roy

No, I don't need you—all I need is what dough I got coming and a chance to pick up my traps and

get out of here.   After the raw deal I got last night
—me keep on working in this shooting gallery?

Nick

Listen, Lane—you gotta work—just tonight——

Roy

(*Turns away*)   What a chance——

Nick

(*Seeing that nothing can be gained this way,*
NICK's *manner changes to one of oily flattery*)   It
ain't for me I ask you to stay—I can get another
hoofer—but it's because of the peoples that come
here especially to see you, see?

Roy

(*Interested*)   What?

Nick

Already big party come in—they ask me how long
before that young fella comes on with that wonderful personality—they say——

Roy

Well, wait a minute—you say that—what kind of
looking people?

Nick

I don't know who they was—very important people—I say, Mr. Lane, he's not in yet, but he's sure
to come because he don't never disappoint his public.

Roy

I never disappointed my public yet.

Nick

That's what I said—— I told 'em about that time in Danbury, Massachusetts. I told 'em what I always said, that you're a real artist and, that no matter what happens I could always count on you, for the very best that's in you.

Roy

Listen, I'll go on tonight.

Nick

Good.

Roy

But I'm leaving at the end of the week—and the doorman can tell anybody that's interested where to find me.

Ruby

Mills Hotel.

Nick

I knew I could count on you, Lane. Now I'll go out in front and see what I can do. Use the big brain figgerin' how to give a show. Lil not here— nor Billie—nor Pearl—I'll be back.

(*Exit to cabaret*)

Roy

They ain't showed up yet, huh?

Ruby

That's how I heard it.

Roy

I wouldn't go back in this dump neither, if I didn't think it was my duty. (RUBY *gives him the bird*) My big chance will come; I figure I might as well be eating while I'm waiting for it. Billie's usually on time—wonder what's keeping her tonight?

Ruby

The same guy that kept her last night.

Roy

Now I ask you, is that nice?

Ruby

You going to worry about her after the royal raspberry she slipped you? She's got you goin' round like a top.

Roy

I'm thinkin' about the good of the show, that's all. Didn't Nick call up the agents to get a gal to shout in Lil's place?

Ruby

Sure, he called 'em, but the agents are no damn good when you want 'em.

Roy

It's me that knows that, Sister.

Ruby

(*Stringing him*) Well, how was the dear old jail?

Roy

That's all right.

Ruby

Come on, spill it, how'd your act go in the night court?

Roy

Aw, that don't concern you.

Ruby

A mysterious guy. Yeah, if Nick hadn't got you off——

Roy

The big baloney never had nothing to do with it; I got myself off.

Ruby

What'd you say to 'em?

Roy

I told 'em a few things.

Ruby

Didn't you even get a fine?

Ro

No, I wouldn't stand for it. I gave 'em a little spiel.

Ruby

I bet you made quite an impression.

187

Roy

I told 'em who I was—there was a guy there had
seen me play on the Poli time; of course that was
in my favor. I gave 'em a rough idea what I
thought of Steve, too. And that cop that was here
—I and him got to be very good friends. He was
wise from the start that that wasn't my gun—just a
stall to get me out.

Ruby

(*Drawing him out*) Go on

Roy

Sure. And it was a stall about them other bulls
laying outside too. He's a smart cop, that fella,
he knows his oats.

Ruby

And then they just turned you loose?

Roy

Well, listen—— (*Comes closer, and lowers
voice*) McCorn told me to keep this under my hat,
but I guess it wouldn't get no further with an old-
time trouper like you——

Ruby

No.

Roy

Listen, they took me to the morgue to indentify
the other guy.

Ruby

Yeah?

Roy

Gee, the way these gangsters pop each other off. Well, I guess it's nothing but a lucky break kept me from occupying the slab right next to him.

(BILLIE *enters back door. She and* ROY *face each other without speaking.* NICK *enters down hall*)

Billie

Ruby——

Ruby

So you decided to come?

Nick

All right—— I won't say anything—go on— get made up.

Billie

I'm terribly sorry—the Trenton train had a break-down.

Ruby

Hah! (*Gets up and starts toward stairs*) She wants to have us believe she's been out to see her mother. God, if I ever seen a professional virgin, she's it.

Nick

Don't start nothing now—things is worse 'nough.

189

Ruby

All right, sweetheart, but Faith, Hope and Charity is waiting here for news—do we give a show tonight or don't we?

Nick

Sure we give a show—we gotta.

Ruby

All right, I'll go up and tell the other inmates. (*To* BILLIE) Come on, Purity.

(RUBY *exits upstairs*—NICK *turns and hurries into the office.* BILLIE *has been waiting, hoping that* ROY *will speak to her—he ignores her and walks to stairs*)

Billie

(*Pleadingly*) Roy. (*He halts*) Roy, I'm terribly glad to find out you didn't get hurt or anything.

Roy

(*Without turning around*) Sure. See you again some time.

Billie

I don't think that's a very nice way to act. All I says was I'm glad you didn't get hurt.

Roy

It's no thanks to you I didn't.

Billie

Everything would have been all right, if you hadn't tried to boss me.

Roy

Well, I'm done trying to boss you now. Course I feel kind-a sorry on account of the act.

Billie

What do you mean?

Roy

On account of its being busted up, I mean.

Billie

(*Weakly*)   Is it busted?

Roy

Sure.

Billie

Oh.

Roy

Of course when a fella's worked like I have to get together the best dancing act in the business, and gets all ready for bookings, he hates to see it go blooey just because a big stiff that's rancid with coin comes along and cops his partner.

Billie

What right have you got to say he's copped me?

Roy

Last night you lied to save him and against me.

Billie

Yes, but I didn't know—you got no right talking that way. All the girls around here are always saying I'm too good—and you're saying I'm too bad. I hate this damn place.

Roy

And another thing, last night you called me a sap in the presence of several witnesses.

Billie

(*Almost in tears*) Oh, shut up. That's what you are.

(NICK *enters from office*)

Nick

All right—all right—get made up.

> (BILLIE *starts upstairs, so agitated that she
> scarcely senses* NICK'S *presence. She pauses
> and leans over the banister*)

Billie

And I'll tell you something else, and it's most likely the last thing I'll ever tell you—the reason I went to my Mother's was to ask her, if a girl was terribly in love with a person, so much it was like regular love at first sight, was it all right to marry 'em even if they was poor,—that's what. Now, how'd you like to go to hell?

(*Exit upstairs*)

Roy

(*Gazes after her dumfounded. Turns to* NICK)
They pick up that language quick around this honky-
tonk.

Nick

She's right. Don't be interfering with her.

Roy

Well, they's a lot of personal things mixed up
here you don't understand. But I'll tip you off to
one thing—my next partner is going to be a man.

Nick

Fine. Now, I want to tell you about something.
(*He sits*) If Steve comes, don't start yowling at
him.

Roy

(*Gives* NICK *a look of mild surprise*) I wouldn't.

Nick

You done it last night.

Roy

I got wise to a lot of things since then—I didn't
know those guys would shoot you right out in public.

Nick

Well, don't argue with him.

Roy

I ain't going to. I don't carry any gatlin' gun.
The Sullivan Act is O. K. with me—— For one

thing I wouldn't think it was fair to you for me to get in any argument with him, 'cause if he put a hole in me, your show'd be out in the alley. Of course, if Mr. Crandall cares to meet me over in the Y.M.C.A. gym, I'd just as leave tell him what I think about him.

Nick

He's all right, Lane. Good customer. Look— last night, the party alone cost him two thousand dollars, you understand?

Roy

I wasn't saying nothing to Steve anyhow—— I was showing Billie the truth about him. He had a fall out of every girl in the place, why couldn't he leave her alone?

Nick

Cause all men like what's hard to get.

Roy

She had the chance of a life time if she'd only have stuck. It's pretty tough after I had a swell double act framed—— Oh well—nobody never got their name in lights by getting discouraged. (*Tries to snap out of his depression*) Say, what I want to ask you, Boss; what we gonna do for a solo in Lil's spot tonight?

Nick

That's what I want to ask you. You sing it.

194

Roy

I might fake up a Mammy song at that.

Nick

Sure. (*Slaps his back*) You'll be the whole show tonight.

Roy

I am every night. If you don't think so, you're crazy. On the level, boss, I don't know what you'd do without me.

> (PORKY *and* LIL *enter back door. They are both lit, which fact they try to cover up with a great deal of dignity*)

Lil

Hello.

Porky

I told you this was the place.

Roy

We been looking for you, Lil.

Lil

I was looking for you too. (*Goes to* NICK *unsteadily*) Shake hands, Nick, and guess who I am.

Nick

Minnie Stew, that's who you are. What I ought to do is slap a good stiff fine onto you.

> (PORKY *bristling*)

Porky

Slap?

(LIL *stops him, forces him into chair, center,
takes hat off and puts in his lap*)

Lil

Don't pay any attention to Nick, Baby, he don't
mean anything—it's just the way these foreigners
talk.

(*Pats his face*)

Nick

Now you are here, would you hurry a little—
please.

Lil

We been hurrying, Nick—we hurried and hurried. We been the longest time getting here, haven't
we, Andrew?

Porky

That's right, dearie.

Nick

For God's sake, where you been? What's happened to you?

Lil

Almost everything—we're married.

(PORKY *goes asleep*)

Roy

Holy Gee.

Nick

What?

196

Lil

That's the reason we're so proud.

Roy

Oh, is that what you are!

Lil

The joke's on you. You'll all have to give us presents and everything.

Nick

Well, going to work tonight?

Lil

Did I return for these purposes?

Nick

(*Helping her toward stairs*) Then go up and lie down. I'll send up some coffee—and we'll find a place in the office for Porky.

Lil

Andrew—if you please——

Nick

All right, Andrew. (*Motions to* Roy *to take* Lil) Go ahead, Lane.

Roy

Come on, Lil, I'll fix you a couch. (*Whispers to* Lil) You ain't got anything on your hip, have you?

197

Lil

Only a birthmark—and you're the first guy that's asked me about it.

(NICK *shakes* PORKY. *He wakes suddenly and protests as* NICK *leads him to office*)

Porky

I think I'm married.

(NICK *and* PORKY *exeunt to office.* NICK *comes right out and goes to cabaret—meantime* ROY *is struggling to get* LIL *upstairs*)

Roy

Come on, Lil—I'll help you.

Lil

I feel so damn foolish.

Roy

Cut it out—lemme help you.

Lil

Sure. You help me and I'll help you.

(*Nearly knocks him downstairs*)

Roy

Behave yourself, will you? You wouldn't want to have anybody say you missed a performance. Come on now, Lil, this is serious business.

(LIL *exits singing.* ROY *stops to pick up her handbag which has fallen in the scuffle*)

(DOLPH *comes in back door*)

Dolph

(*To* ROY)   Hello, nut—where's Nick?

Roy

Find out, wise guy—I dance here. I ain't a
waiter. (*Exits to dressing room*)

> (DOLPH *is followed in by* STEVE, *who is evi-
> dently laboring under considerable repressed
> excitement.* JOE *comes in from hall with
> coffee and crosses to stairs*)

Joe

Good evening, Mr. Crandall.

Steve

Hello, Joe. (*To* DOLPH) Get outside and do as
I told you. (DOLPH *goes out back door.* STEVE
follows JOE) Listen, Joe—I'm not here to anyone
tonight. Get that. And tip me if McCorn or any
dick blows in. (JOE *starts to leave*) Wait a second. Don't be in such a hurry. Here— (*He
hands* JOE *a bill*)

Joe

Thanks, Mr. Crandall.

Steve

And tell the doorman to turn away anybody he
don't know,—and give him this. (*Hands* JOE *another bill.* JOE *grins*) Some of Scar Edwards'
playmates might try to crash in looking for trouble.

(NICK *comes in from hall*) I got my own lookout men planted, but I'm taking no chances.

Nick

Hurry along with that, Joe. (JOE *goes upstairs*) Hello, Steve. (JOE *exits upstairs*) What's the matter? You look sick.

Steve

(*He has lost his hard assurance—he is nervous— his face almost twitches—he can't stand still. He speaks very quietly*) I ain't feeling as well as I could.

Nick

No?

Steve

(*Takes off his hat*) Look at that lid.

Nick

Huh?

Steve

Look at that hole?

Nick

Sure, I see it—Cigarette?

Steve

No—bullet.

Nick

(*Impressed*) For God's sake.

Steve

Just a minute ago. I'm standing down here in the middle of the block—in front of the Midtown Garage talking to Dolph, when buzz—(*Puts hat on*) it goes through my hat.

Nick

Mmm! (*To show his concern*) Who done it?

Steve

That's the hell of it. I don't know.

Nick

I mean, where'd it come from?

Steve

That's what I'm telling you—there wasn't a sound—whoever took a crack at me must of had a silencer on his gat—

Nick

(*Guttural exclamation*) Ohoo!

Steve

There wasn't anyone on the street—that is, anyone but what seemed to be walking along minding his own business—but just as the shot went through my lid, a taxicab across the street started up and went toward Sixth Avenue like a bat out of hell—but there was only a woman in it.

Nick

A woman?

Steve

Yeh—it couldn't been her—I don't think. It must have come from some of those windows on the second floor—Scar Edwards' mob, I guess—they use silencers—

Nick

Whoo—that's bad, Steve—extra bad.

Steve

An inch lower and it would have been a lot worse. It's good I planned to get out of here when I did.

Nick

You goin' tonight?

Steve

Yeh. (*Walks toward back door—restless*) Get me a drink, will you? (NICK *goes into office and comes out with bottle.* JOE *comes downstairs and goes toward hall*) Joe—don't forget to give that bill to the doorman.

Joe

No, sir. (*Exits to hall as* NICK *returns from office with glass and bottle*)

Nick

Where you going?

Steve

(*Comes to* NICK—*takes drink*) I'll lay in with some friends up in Montreal for the time being.

(PEARL *enters back door. She comes in fearfully, sees them and pulls herself together.* STEVE *turns quickly at sound of door—but seeing who it is, relaxes again*)

Nick

About time!

Steve

(*Perfunctorily*) Hello, Pearl.

Nick

Hurry up, you're late, don't waste any time.
(PEARL *hurries upstairs*)

Nick

If you didn't croak Scar Edwards, what you blowin' for?

Steve

(*Walking away from him*) I can make my plans without your help, Nick.

Nick

Sure. (*Watches him*) You taking Billie with you?

Steve

That's some more of your business.

Nick

I want to know if I gotta get a new gal, that's all.

Steve

(*Crosses to* NICK, *who pours another drink and passes it to him*) Well, I'm taking her all right, but she don't know it yet, so you don't need to advertise. I prefer to get 'em without being rough —but I'm pressed for time, so I'll have to try Dolph's stuff this crack. (*Drinks*) Now I gotta get hold of Porky.

Nick

He's here.

Steve

He is?

Nick

In there. Drunker than hell—he got married.

Steve

He got what?

Nick

Sure, to Lil. They both come in while ago stewed to the gills.

Steve

To Lil? Gee! Well, will you tell me why he fell for that big horse?

Nick

Maybe she ain't your kind—but them big broads that's been all through the war sometimes make pretty women at home.

Steve

Oh, I ain't boosting for Porky—at that, I think Lil got the worst of it. Let's take a lamp at him, I want to see what he looks like married.

(As they start to enter office, STEVE sees BILLIE coming downstairs. He gestures to NICK to go ahead. NICK exits—STEVE comes back to meet BILLIE)

Hello, beautiful. Well, you look as sweet as sugar —How's tricks?

Billie

All right. (BILLIE *is ill at ease with him. She hurries up to the table with her props, trying to be casual, but betraying a new manner toward* STEVE, *that almost amounts to suspicion*) I came in late and then I hurried so—that I'm about the first one ready.

Steve

Found the folks all right, did you?

Billie

Oh, fine.

Steve

That's good. That gives me a great deal of pleasure. Of course we missed not having you stay for the finish of the party last night.

Billie

Well, you were awfully nice about letting me go home, Mr. Crandall.

Steve

Well, I'll tell you, Billie girl, any time I'm not nice, you remind me and I'll get nice, 'cause as far

as you're concerned, that's the way I want to be,
see?

Billie

Of course I don't understand about the detective
and everything.

Steve

Of course you don't, Girlie, but I'll explain it
to you. It's just politics—that's all. I'll tell you
all about it after the show tonight. It'll be very
interesting. You're going for a ride with me tonight
you know.

Billie

Well, I don't know. (*He has taken her hand, she
draws it away, as tho by accident, and steps back*)

Steve

You haven't forgotten. That was a promise—
you wouldn't try to go back on that.

Billie

Well—

Steve

(*Quite frantic*) You did promise—don't forget
that—

Billie

I wouldn't go back on my promise—
   (MAZIE *enters on stairs*)

Mazie

Hello, Steve.

206

Steve

(*Mutters*) Hello, Mazie. (MAZIE'S *presence drives him away. He starts for office then turns back and touches her arm as tho he wanted to assure himself that she were still there—almost reverently*) Don't forget now—(*Exits to office*)

Mazie

(*Comes downstairs*) I see he's still friends.

(RUBY *enters stairs*)

(ROY *and* GIRLS *come downstairs. They all wear the costumes for opening number as in Act I*)

Ruby

Yeh, she promised to come early and shave my neck.

(NICK *enters from office*)

Mazie

Well, here we are for the merry-merry.

Nick

Now remember, some pep tonight.

Mazie

I'm full of pep and no control.

Roy

Save your pep, kid—you may need it. (*Goes to cabaret doors—he steps out*) Good evening, folks. (*The doors close behind him*)

Ruby

If that's pep, I never smelled gin.

Mazie

Listen, Dizzy—you won't smell anything again—
'cause I'm going to bust your smeller. (*She starts*)

Billie

Mazie, behave yourself.

Grace

What is this, Grand Street?

Ann

My head aches.

Ruby

Wait till the show's over—I'll show you.

(BILLIE *pulls* MAZIE. GRACE *holds* RUBY)

Mazie

Why wait?

(ROY *comes back from cabaret and pushes between them*)

Roy

That's enough of this. You can't go out there
scrapping like that. I don't want my stuff spoiled.
I got friends out there—agents and managers—
looking me over every night.

Mazie

Oh, I forgot—I ain't used to working with these
headline acts.

Roy

Well, there's lots worse than me headlining, sister—

Mazie

Well, for Gawd sake, what did I say?

(*Buzzer sounds—lights flash*)

Roy

Come on—quit it—line up. Let's unravel our daily dozen. Every night's a first night. Give 'em your best.

> (*The music swells as the doors open and they dance out. As* Roy *is going thru the doors,* Steve *enters from office—*Roy *thumbs his nose at him and exits*)

Steve

(*Looks out after him*) You'd think last night would a-took all the freshness out of that hoofer, wouldn't you?

Nick

Huh—forget it. I'm going to fire him.

Steve

You don't need to bother—I'll tend to him myself when I get the time. I don't want to have it happen too quick after his visit with McCorn. (*Moves about nervously*) He hasn't been around tonight, has he?

Nick

Who?

Steve

McCorn.

Nick

No. Why? You want to see him?

Steve

That's just what I don't want to do. I thought he might come snoopin' around again.

Nick

You afraid of him—Dan McCorn?

Steve

Me? What for? He ain't got nothing on me—not a thing.

Nick

Sure he ain't—so why get excited?

Steve

Well, I'll tell you, Nicholas—a guy like McCorn gets on my nerve—he don't say anything—he don't make any accusations, but that damn rotten slow way of talking he's got, and that dirty smile—you know—sorta gets me ragged. Now what the hell did he want to take my gun for last night?

Nick

Well, after all, Steve, none of us ain't got no right to carry a gat—

Lil

(*Comes from dressing room, starts downstairs*)
Where's my husband?

(STEVE *looks her over and shakes his head and
exits to office*)

Nick

He's all right, Lil.

Lil

Tell him his little wife—No, I'll tell him myself.

(*She finds that coming downstairs backward
is lots easier*)

Nick

Feel better now, Lil? All ready for going on?

Lil

Say, Nick, please can I cut my first number? I
can do it, if I have to, but I ain't just set.

Nick

(*Resigned*) All right—go on out—sit down, drink
some more black coffee and see the show.

Lil

Thanks, old timer—you're a true friend. That's
just what I said to Andrew—I says, if ever your
little Lillie had a true friend—it's that greasy
Greek, Nick Verdis.

(PORKY *enters from office*)

(LIL *crosses to* PORKY)
I'm going out and see the show, darling.

Porky

I'll go with you, dearie.

Lil

Take my arm, sweetheart, and keep the hell off my feet.

(*They exeunt to cabaret*)

(GIRLS *and* ROY *come in from cabaret.* GIRLS *put props on table*)

Roy

Well, we ruined 'em, Boss—

Nick

Listen, Lane, Lil ain't able to work—I gotta find something to fill that spot.

Roy

Better give 'em an orchestra specialty.

Nick

They'll get sick of that too before the night's over. Listen, I been thinking—I'll take a chance—how'd you like to break in your act with Billie—huh?

Roy

(MAZIE *pokes* BILLIE, *and the girls show interest*)

What?

Nick

You can do it for the next number.

Roy

No—the act is split—it's off—all busted up.

Nick

Listen, you been talkin' about it—rehearsin' and everything—now I give you a chance—

Roy

I'd like to do it for you, Boss, but I ain't got a partner.

Nick

(*To* BILLIE) What's the matter? You won't work?

Billie

I didn't say I wouldn't. He don't want me any more.

Nick

(*To* BILLIE) Go on. (*She runs upstairs, excited and happy*) Just because I need the two of you, you're busted up. This is a chance for you. Come on, I ask it for special favor. There's a orchestra number first, so you got lots of time. I'll give the agent a good report, no matter how rotten it is.

Roy

As long as Miss Moore wants to do it I'm willing to, just to keep the show going.

Nick

Fine. (*To others*) We'll do the Hawaiian number after that.

(*The girls start to break up—some going toward stairs, others to tables to put down props*)

Roy

We didn't rehearse to-day.

(Roy *starts warming up with some dance steps*)

Mazie

Can we go out to the tables and watch, Mr. Verdis?

Nick

Sure, go ahead.

Ruby

(*Going upstairs*) They'll die standing up.

Mazie

(*As* PEARL *starts upstairs*) Come on, Pearl, and watch 'em, why don't you?

Pearl

I'll change first and be right out.

Roy

Mazie, tell Brophy to play my introduction music when this orchestra number is over—he'll know what you mean.

Mazie

Sure.

(*Exeunt* MAZIE, GRACE *and* ANN *to hall.* NICK *takes pencil and paper and plans his pro-*

gram. Roy *in the midst of his dancing suddenly gets a thought. He walks over to* Nick
importantly)

Roy

Boss, there's gotta be a better understanding
about the money in the future—

Nick

Maybe after you do this act you have no future.
(*Laughs*)

Roy

Razzin' me, eh? All right, after tonight you
gotta struggle along without me. How do you like
them grapes?

Nick

Aw, you can't take a joke. You and me, Lane,
we'se friends. Go on now, like a good fellow.
Maybe I'll have a sign fixed with your name in
lights.

Roy

Well, how big a sign?

Nick

I'll tell you after I see the act. (*Exits to hall*)
(Billie *enters stairs*)

Billie

We might as well go on and try it, now that we
rehearsed it so much, even if you don't like me any
more.

Roy

(*Hooking her dress*) It isn't a question of liking you. But when I get a throw-down like last night, I get wise to myself.

Billie

Well, when I get a throw-down like I just got today, I'm wise to myself too. But lots of people that don't like each other, they still work together. I mean, if you still think we'd make a good team, then it's just a business proposition. A couple can be in the same act without being crazy about each other.

Roy

Well, I used to think we'd make about the best combo I could imagine—but I'm the kind of a guy I don't want to butt in where I ain't wanted. (*Sniffs*) You want to run over a few of them steps? (BILLIE *nods*) Just remember your routine, that's all you got to do.

Billie

Let's try the finish—that's where we got mixed up at the last rehearsal.

Roy

All you gotta do is follow me. Watch me out the corner of your eye and you can't go wrong. (*Takes place to do steps. She puts arms around*

*his neck, pulling their cheeks together. He takes
her hand away and places it at waist)* **Down** here.

Billie

The last time we did it this way.

Roy

Well, that was the last time. We'll do it now
the old way. (*Stops acting and looks away from
her*) You see, it's kinda spoiled it for me, thinkin'
you might have had your arms around Steve that
way.

Billie

I haven't. (*Pause*) And when I lied last night
about the drunken man, it was because I had promised Steve to say that, and I didn't know a thing
about that you'd said the opposite. And I went
home alone last night.

Roy

(*Looks at her—melts*) We'll do the finish the
new way—like this. (*Puts her arm around his
neck*) Billie, you know that, what you asked your
mother when you went home today—about marryin'
a poor fellow?

Billie

Yeah—

Roy

Well. (*Buzzer. They jump apart*) Never mind.
You can tell me later. We gotta think of our work

now. On your toes, baby—don't get nervous. (*At door*) Listen, Mr. Verdis is makin' an announcement—sensational newcomers—Roy Lane and Company—Oh Boy, don't that make you feel proud?

Billie

(*Overcome with sudden panic*)   Roy — I'm scared—

Roy

Don't be scared—remember I'm right beside you. It'll all be over before you know it.

Billie

Roy, I don't believe I can go on. Can't we wait till tomorrow till we have a chance to rehearse?

Roy

Pull yourself together. We can't have no stage fright gummin' our act. I'll give you a sock in a minute. There's our music. We'll finish in a blaze of glory. (*Pulls her to entrance—blesses himself*) Lots of snap now. We'll show 'em. Let's go.

(*They exit to cabaret, dancing gaily*)

(DAN MCCORN *enters hall*. JOE *follows*)

Joe

No strangers allowed back here—Mister.

Dan

That's all right Aloy-ious. I'm no stranger.

Joe

Well, you can't—
(NICK *comes in from other end of hall*)

Dan

Oh yes I can—

Joe

No, you can't.

Nick

Joe! (*Signals him to go*)
(JOE *exits to hall sulkily*)

Dan

Evening, Nick.

Nick

What you doin' back here?

Dan

Just thought I'd drop in and say hello. Steve around?

Nick

Nope, I ain't seen him all day.

Dan

He'll be in later, though, won't he?

Nick

(*Sits.*) No—he won't come tonight. He had such a big night last night—y'understand. You want to see him?

Dan

Nothing in particular. They'll be lots of other chances. Have a good time last night?

Nick

No, them kinda things make me sick. You gotta do it, understand, but it ain't no fun. When I get drunk for pleasure, that's one thing—but when I get drunk for business, daugh! No—no.

Dan

Sure. All the girls stay?

Nick

Yes, I guess so. I don't know. I got cock-eyed awful soon. I ain't sure of nothing last night.

Dan

Well, guess I'll blow. My partner's waiting for me outside.

Nick

Is he waiting like them other bulls you told Steve about last night?

Dan

(*Smiles*) No, he's waiting.

Nick

You're a pretty slick guy, Mac—you put it over on me, too.

Dan

(*Still smiling*) Oh, you're all wrong, Nick—they were there.

Nick

Yea, like hell. Well, it's all right with me—put me in awful bad—them Chicagoes started everything.

Dan

That's a bad bunch a bail-hoppers, Nick. On the level, I could a grabbed a couple of 'em—but it wouldn't get me anything. We don't want 'em here in New York.

Nick

Steve tells me they're goin' back to Chicago in a couple of days—

Dan

I thought you said you didn't see Steve all day?

Nick

(*Pause—caught*) I didn't—he called me on the phone—he told me—

Dan

Oh! (*Pause*) Well, see you later.

Nick

You coming round again?

Dan

Oh, I don't mean tonight.

Nick

Well, that's good. You're a fine fellow, Mac, but every time you come in my cabaret, about twenty people goes out.

Dan

You got nothing to fear from me, Nick.

(RUBY *and* PEARL *enter from dressing rooms. They have changed to next chorus costume— they come down the stairs*)

Nick

I know that, but it looks bad when you're round so much.

Ruby

My Gawd, this place is getting like Headquarters —every time you come into a room around here, you fall over a badge.

Nick

Mac's just visiting. Besides, you shut up.

Ruby

(*Going toward hall*) Is that act out there so bad you can't look at it?

Dan

(*As* PEARL *crosses toward cabaret*) Hello there.

Pearl

Hello.

(*Girls exeunt to cabaret*)

Dan

She's still around, huh?

Nick

Why not?

Dan

I thought that party last night would be too much for her.

Nick

These kids I got are tanks—they can drink any ten men under.

Dan

Well, be good. I'll take a peek at this new act of yours. (*Exits to hall*)

(NICK *peeks out to be sure* DAN *is not coming back.* STEVE *has opened office door slowly. He comes out; almost twitching with nervousness*)

Steve

God damn him, what does he want?

Nick

Nothing important, he says. Just asked for you. I said you wasn't here like you told me.

Steve

He's got nothing on me. Not a thing—

(PEARL *walks down hall quickly, just glancing in as she passes double doors and disappears*)

Nick

Say, listen, what the hell's the matter with you? Soon as somebody mentions this dick McCorn, you go up in the air. What's the reason for this?

Steve

I'm all shot, I tell you. Too much booze last night, I guess, and—Oh, a lot of things—(*There is a noise of someone trying back door under stairs, then a knock.* STEVE *rises, controls himself and sits again*) Take a look first!

Nick

(*Peeks out*) It's Dolph.

    (NICK *unbolts the door, opens it.* DOLPH *enters*)

Steve

What's the matter?

Dolph

(*Frightened*) Why—I—a—

Steve

What the hell is it?

Dolph

There's a guy out there been walking up and down—passed by a dozen times—makes me all nervous.

Steve

A dick?

Dolph

Either that or one of Scar Edwards' bunch—nobody I seen before.

Nick

There's a lot of people walk up and down—it's a free country almost. What's to be afraid of? You guys ain't done nothing.

Dolph

Ain't there some way for you to get out of here, Steve—now—before—

Steve

No, I'm not ready yet. I'll break cover in an hour. Go on, wait out there.

Dolph

But it ain't safe out there. One of the Edwards crowd might take a shot at me, with a silencer.

Steve

Go on out—stick by that back entrance like I told you to. You're my right hand man, ain't you?
(*Slaps him on back. Pushes him out*)

Dolph

Sure! All right.
(*Exits out back door.* STEVE *closes door and bolts it*)

Nick

I don't get this business, Steve.

Steve

Listen, Nick, you and I been best kind of pals for a long time. I'd shoot the works for you and I hope you would for me.

Nick

Sure I would. What you want?

Steve

I'm going to blow tonight. I don't want to have any slips. This damn bull McCorn is getting too curious. He thinks some of my mob got Edwards.

Nick

Did they?

Steve

No, they didn't. Now listen, I want you to get Joe or someone you can trust to beat it over to Charlie's and tell him to bring his car, not mine, they know mine—and leave it at the back entrance for me.

Nick

You can phone him.

Steve

No, these dicks might have the wires tapped. Sending Joe is safer. After the show, I'll take Billie and a couple of these broads and pile in the car. Looks like we're going for a joy ride, savvy? Then if they trail us, when I get 'em out on the Post

Road, I can lose 'em, see, but they won't think I'm going to blow, so long as I got the girls with me. I can get rid of the ones I don't want later on.

Nick

You go to lots of trouble just 'cause a bull's asking questions. My Gawd, Steve, where's your guts?

Steve

You think I'm yellow, huh? I don't want no man thinking that. Listen, Nick. (*Takes him roughly by wrist and comes close*) I did that job myself. (NICK *motions quiet with both hands*) Now, they can't get me for it—they got nothing on me but that gun—but it's getting on my nerves —I'm getting ragged and I want to get out of here. Now, have you got it?

Nick

Sure, I understand. But don't bump nobody else off in here.

Steve

You won't get in trouble—I'll fix that. Now send for the car.

Nick

Sure, right away—you wait in the office, Steve. (*He hurries into cabaret.* STEVE *goes to big door under stairs, peeks out cautiously through peep hole—then crosses to cabaret*

*doors, closes them. As he does so, the party
door opens, and* PEARL *steps in with a pistol
in her hand. It has a silencer affixed*)

Pearl

(*Low*) Turn around, Rat! (*He wheels about*)
I don't want to give it to you like you did him—
in the back.

Steve

(*He can't move*) For Christ's sake, don't!

Pearl

I'm giving you more chance than you gave him—
I'm looking at you—and the last thing you see before you go straight to hell is Jim Edwards' woman,
who swore to God she'd get you.

Steve

(*Backing away*) Don't—don't kill me—don't—

Pearl

Whine, you rat—I knew you would.

(*She fires. There is just a pish as the gun goes
off, a slight curl of smoke.* STEVE *lurches
toward office and falls out of sight as he
clutches at the door.* PEARL *stands paralyzed
by the violence of her act. Then she thrusts
the pistol into her handbag and scurries upstairs like a frightened rabbit. Before she*

is out of sight RUBY *opens the cabaret doors and comes in laughing derisively*)

Ruby

Ha! A total loss!
(*The other girls follow down hall as* BILLIE *and* ROY *rush in from cabaret. There is some applause*)

Mazie

Them guys don't know a good act when they see it.

Roy

Come on, Billie, it's good for a bow.
(BILLIE *and* ROY *run back*)

Ruby

And they even steal a bow.

Ann

And they rehearsed it, too.
(BILLIE *and* ROY *enter*)

Billie

How do you think it went?

Grace

That bunch are full of novocaine.

Ruby

You'd be a riot in the Palace.

Roy

We could have grabbed another. That detective and Nick crabbed our act with their argument. How could we get attention, everybody watching them. Gee, what a rotten break. Well, go on up, kids, make your change. I'll give the leader a buzz —see how they like it.

(*He exits to hall while girls start upstairs*)

Billie

I did my best.

Mazie

Sure you did, kid, cheer up. I don't think it's as bad as they say it is.

(*The girls go out.* DAN *and* NICK *are heard arguing. They enter from hall*)

Nick

Dan, you're getting me sore, y' understand—I gotta right to send any of my waiters any place I want—without any advice from you.

Dan

(*Pulling him around*) Now listen to me, Greek— I been pretty nice to you in a lotta ways—now you get this—you don't want to be accused of helping some guy that's wanted for murder, do you?

Nick

No, but I—

Dan

Then listen to me; before you do any more for
Steve Crandall I want to have a talk with him; and
after that you can do as you please. I been waiting around here until your show was over before
I started anything—because I didn't want to give
your dump any worse name than it's got. So keep
out of my business and you won't have to sit in a
witness chair. Now, I happen to know Steve's
here. Come on; where is he? Where is he?
(NICK *motions his head toward office*) Tell him
I want to see him. (NICK *goes reluctantly to office.
He opens door and draws back with a gasp*)
What's the matter? (*Dan runs to door, sizes up
situation, and steps past him into the room*) Come
in. Shut the door. (*They go to office.* NICK *fearfully—the door is shut*)

(RUBY *enters, half dressed, followed by* MAZIE,
*who catches her on stairs and chokes her—
bending her over the banisters*)

Mazie

Now you're going to eat mud.

Ruby

Quit.

Mazie

Now what am I the son of?

231

Ruby

You're an angel.

Mazie

Say uncle—

Ruby

Uncle.

Mazie

(*Releases her*) Now, get back, I'd drop you over if I wasn't feeling so good natured.

(RUBY *exits.* MAZIE *dusts off her hands as* ROY *enters with a rush. He has supper card in his hand*)

Roy

Look, Mazie—look at this—I got this from Mike Shea—he just caught our act.

Mazie

Who's he?

Roy

He's one of the biggest booking agents in New York—he wrote me on this supper card—

Mazie

Mike Shea? Never heard of him—

Roy

(*At top of stairs*) Listen, what he wrote. At last I got a break. "I can offer you and partner

Chambersburgh and Pottsville next week—"
Billie, Billie.

(*Runs out to dressing rooms*)

Mazie

(*Laughs*) That's one for the book! (*Follows him*)

(NICK *comes out of office, looking under great stress—*DAN *follows*)

Dan

He's dead all right. (NICK *moans*) Right thru the old pump.

Nick

(*Turning back to him—suddenly alive*) Lane! The hoofer! He's the one. He killed Steve. I'll betcha. He was out to get him.

Dan

The actor, you mean?

(PEARL *enters on stairs—she starts down—hears the voices and halts*)

Nick

Sure! He's been tryin' to get him. He's been lyin' about him.

Dan

No, it wasn't Lane—it was suicide.

233

Nick

Suicide?

Dan

Sure. (*Fascinated,* PEARL *comes slowly down stairs, her. hands against the back wall.* DAN *talks to* NICK, *his eye on the girl*) Here's Steve's own gun—with one chamber empty.

Nick

I thought you had that?

Dan

I gave it back to Steve today.

Nick

But Steve said—

Dan

I said I gave it back to him today. He knew I was going to pinch him, so he took the shortest way out. I'm calling up headquarters to report it suicide—so that's what it is.

Nick

All right—all right—whatever you say.

Dan

Give me the key to this door. (NICK *gives him key to the door;* DAN *locks it.* PEARL *sinks to the chair by piano*) I want to keep everyone out of there till the Coroner gets here. I'll wait for him out back. (*He starts to back door; as he passes*

234

PEARL *he speaks disinterestedly—out of the corner of his mouth*) Pull yourself together, kid.

(*Exits back door*)

(PEARL *lets her head fall forward, weak with relief, as* DAN *exits and the other girls and* ROY *enter on stairs, laughing and joking excitedly*)

Mazie

Pottsville and Chambersburgh, Gawd, Billie, you must love this guy.

Billie

I certainly do.

Roy

I been so busy gettin' the act framed, I ain't had time to show you how much I love you. But here goes.

(ROY *and* BILLIE *embrace*)

Ann

My Gawd, in front of everybody—

Grace

When do you two play the matrimonial circuit—

Mazie

Break! Time!

Ruby

Look at 'em.

(GIRLS *laughing and pulling* BILLIE *and* ROY *apart*)

235

Nick

(*Bursting out suddenly—his nerves unable to stand their hilarity*)   Cut out this noise—I—ah—we gotta cut it out, y' understand.

(*They stand dumfounded by his violence. The buzzer sounds—and* Roy *snaps back to his job*)

Roy

There goes the gong, girls.   All ready!   Come on, Pearl.   Gee, I'm happy.   Our names will be in bright lights soon.   Roy Lane and Co.   Remember you're all artists.   Here we go—here we go—

(*The girls form in line and dance into cabaret singing as* Nick *crosses himself and prays leaning against the door as though half fainting*)

CURTAIN